PRAISE FOR
PURPOSE FORWARD

"*Purpose Forward* is an important contribution to not only high school seniors and college students but to anyone who is looking for a roadmap toward self-discovery. Page after page, the reader will find useful, cohesive and research-supported tools to confidently advance forward; with genuineness, with authenticity, and with purpose."

—Marie T. Rogers, Ph.D., RYT,
author of *Life in Focus: A Self-Discovery
Journal for Powerful Transformation*

"*Ideal* for today's workforce and career changers as they search for meaning through self-awareness."

—Dr. Kim Stack, executive director for
undergraduate student success and academic
support at University of Rhode Island

"During these times of rapid change and uncertainty, *Purpose Forward* is a reliable guidebook filled with assurance and pragmatic advice."

—Dave Ursillo Jr., mental health clinician,
coach, and author

"Purpose Forward is the perfect book for anyone who wants a light read with exercises that will teach them how to find and create their purpose."

—Jamie Mocrazy, keynote speaker, resilience advocate, & founder of MoCrazy Foundation

"Purpose Forward is jam-packed with actionable advice and journal prompts that will help readers of any age navigate their career path.

—Elana Lyn Gross, M.S., content manager & editor at Monster, bestselling author of *What Next?: Your Five-Year Plan for Life After College*

PURPOSE
FORWARD

THE ULTIMATE CAREER STARTER'S GUIDE TO FINDING A CAREER (AND LIFE) OF PURPOSE

MELISSA M. CARVALHO, M.A., RYT

Published by Illuminated Path Press

Cover design, interior design and images by Streetlight Graphics
Edited by Daniel Tortora

www.melissamcarvalho.com

DEDICATION

This book is dedicated to my mother, Mary Jaroma Misiaszek, for living a life of wild devotion to her passions.

It is because of you I learned what life purpose truly is.

TABLE OF CONTENTS

INTRODUCTION

WHY WE NEED TO FIND OUR PURPOSE

"The purpose of life is to discover your gift. The work of life is to develop it. The meaning of life is to give your gift away."

—William Shakespeare

WELCOME!

I F YOU'RE LIKE MOST HUMANS, when you started your educational journey, you were full of dreams about a future filled with success and fulfillment. Like countless others, you believed that this academic pilgrimage held the golden key to unlocking the doors to a fabulous job and a career that would make your parents (or children) proud!

It seemed like the way ahead would be smooth, effortless, and full of unlimited potential.

But the actual journey didn't go as planned. It has been filled with uncertainty and doubt (and maybe even accompanied by some unwelcome knots in your stomach). Your big dreams began to collide with the reality of setbacks and unexpected turns. What used to be clear goals are now hidden behind large clouds of confusion. The path to your perfect future became a twisty road filled with stress, some crazy curve balls, and pains-taking moments of questioning your choices.

It's natural to feel disheartened by the gap between your expectations and the reality in front of you.

You may find yourself in any number of stages in your career arc. Perhaps you are

- Immersed in your high school journey

- Progressing through your college venture

- Gainfully employed but considering a career change

- Re-creating and finding yourself after the transition to motherhood

Graduation day may have already come and gone, or maybe you are staring dreamingly at the date circled on the calendar while curled up in your microfiber fleece blanket. You may be paralyzed by indecision, uncertain of how to leverage your major, or overwhelmed by waaaaaay too many or too few career options.

You may be one of the fortunate souls who got to start their job on the Monday after graduation. Perhaps that job brought you some happiness or presented its own set of challenges. You may still be searching for the right job, or you could be contemplating a complete shift in your career path altogether. You may even be looking to stay in your current role but yearn for greater meaning.

Are you getting any heat from family and friends, urging you to "figure it out"—and stat?! Financial obligations such as student loans, providing for your loved ones, or simply managing everyday expenses like car insurance while planning a trip to Costa Rica may give you some anxiety.

You want to learn how to set yourself apart in this fiercely competitive job market, are digesting your internship experience and wondering where you go from here, or are confronting the challenge of not having much real-world work experience yet.

Wherever you may find yourself on your career and purpose journey, I am here to support you. Like a warm hug from a good friend.

Know that you are exactly where you are meant to be. Confusion and disappointment can often be the grounds on which inspiration and opportunity can develop. This book is meant to be that spark that catalyzes that uncertainty and transforms it into clarity and action.

I am genuinely so glad you are here. And I have very high hopes for you!

Because regardless of what you have already experienced or are yet to experience, it is time to venture forward. It's time to Purpose Forward, my friend!

Because purpose is much more than finding a job, or even a career. It is about discovering the deeper meaning and fulfillment in everything we do, aligning our actions with our values, and making a positive impact on the world around us. It is about understanding and living life in a meaningful way, having clarity in who we are, and having purposeful intention in the pathways we choose. Purpose is about recognizing that our time in this world is a precious gift and squeezing the most out of it that we possibly can. If this is a mindset that resonates with you, trust me, you are in the right place.

Now let's chat about two generations of folks who *especially* have a collective interest in purpose.

HOW GEN Z AND MILLENNIALS ARE SHAKING IT UP

Work has always represented some balance between the pursuit of happiness weighed against the practical needs of survival. Previous generations did not always have the luxury of finding joy and fulfillment in the daily grind of making ends meet. Those who loved what they did day in and day out were considered fortunate, as this was not the case for many.

But things are shifting. Over the years, people have come to expect more than just a paycheck from the place where they spend the bulk of their waking hours. According to recent surveys (September 7, 2022) conducted by McKinsey and Company in the article "The Search for 'Meaning' at Work" by Kate Morgan, 82 percent of employees believe it's important their company has a purpose. And 70 percent of employees say their personal sense of purpose is defined by their work and rank purpose as more important than pay, and "when that work feels meaningful, they perform better, and are much more committed and are about half as likely to go looking for a new job."

The younger generations (Gen Z—those born between 1995 and 2010 and Millennials—born between 1981 and 1995), more so than the generations before them, view their vocation not just as work and pay but as a means of personal fulfillment, joy, and meaning. We no longer want to just get by; we want to find passion in our craft and truly thrive. There are many possible reasons for this generational shift that we won't be able to fully explore here. But some possible explanations include the following:

Greater Emphasis on Higher Education: In recent decades, there has been a cultural shift towards valuing higher education as a means to a successful and fulfilling career. More people are attending college and pursuing advanced degrees, which often leads to higher expectations for job satisfaction and meaningful work.

Exposure to Diverse Career Options: With the internet and social media, individuals have greater access to information about various careers and opportunities worldwide. This exposure expands their awareness of potential paths and encourages them to explore careers that resonate with their passions and aspirations.

Melissa M. Carvalho, M.A., RYT

Work-Life Integration: Millennials and Gen Z value work-life integration over traditional work-life balance. They seek careers that align with their personal values and passions, allowing them to find fulfillment in both their professional and personal lives.

Technological Empowerment: Advancements in technology have empowered individuals to pursue independent ventures and creative careers. Social media and online platforms enable people to research and share their passions and reach a global audience, making it easier to build careers around meaningful pursuits.

Shift in Definition of Success: Success is no longer solely defined by wealth and material possessions; it is increasingly associated with personal growth, contribution, and leaving a positive legacy.

Pandemic Reflection: The COVID-19 pandemic was a transformative event that prompted people to reevaluate their priorities and career choices. It highlighted the importance of essential workers and inspired many to seek careers that make a positive impact on society and public health.

Mental Health Awareness: Younger generations are more open about mental health issues and understand the importance of having fulfilling and purposeful work for overall well-being.

Regardless of the reasons, it is clear that the working world, particularly the emerging young workforce, has come to the consensus that it's not enough to have a job that just pays the bills and gives us health insurance. I mean, it works—we can get by. But is that truly the narrative we wish to tell, dedicating a staggering 2,080 hours or more each year to just getting by?

While that may be sufficient for some, personally, I dare to dream of a life that transcends mere survival. I know you do, too.

Life without purpose is like a ship without a rudder. Just as a ship relies on its rudder to chart its course through questionable seas, so too do we depend on that guiding force, that unwavering "purpose," to steer us towards our desired destination. We can work in meager jobs, navigate the formulaic trajectory of a career, or follow a predetermined path, but it is in the pursuit of a personally rewarding career path that aligns with our life purpose that the true magic unfolds—a transformative shift from mere contentment to truly flourishing.

It is with this understanding in mind that this book exists—integrated wisdom crafted to illuminate the path towards a life that transcends mediocrity. It's your guide to embarking on a transformative journey of self-discovery and deep personal growth.

This is the right program and book for you if you are

- ✓ Finding yourself wondering why some people are thriving and living their purpose and others aren't sure how to begin (maybe this is you!)

- ✓ Feeling stuck and wanting to get yourself from point A to point B so you can thrive and reach your potential

- ✓ Needing to get more in touch with who you are at your core—your passions, values, and strengths—and uncover where your life journey is heading

- ✓ Wanting to learn how to explore your purpose from a holistic perspective, integrating mind, body, and spirit

Within these pages, I'll help you discover precious kernels of knowledge embedded within you, nudging the needle ever closer to a purposeful existence and a deeply fulfilling career.

ABOUT ME

I'm not just writing this book as a recruiter & life purpose/career coach. I am writing it as a fellow human being (and millennial!) who weathered her own arduous journey in the search for meaningful work.

About a decade ago, after dedicating an entire 10 years to the recruiting and human resources professions, I found myself at a crossroads. The kind with a speeding train coming at me. It was a disheartening realization. The organizations I had chosen left me empty, burnt out, and, frankly, depressed. I had a shift in mindset regarding what I was willing to tolerate and realized that I needed a change ASAP for my well-being!

To make a long story short, after much agonizing, I made the decision to change my entire career trajectory and took a risk. Despite a monumental 30 percent pay cut (which was a massive financial and lifestyle change!), I accepted a role in career development within a nonprofit—a pursuit that held deep meaning for me. This conscious decision became a major catalyst in my career, allowing me to embrace a life that aligned more closely with my highest purpose. Taking this risk reinforced the importance of living in alignment with my core truths, pursuing meaningful work within an organization I could be proud of, and surrounding myself with individuals who supported and nurtured my growth (many of whom are dear friends of mine today!)

I am immensely grateful for the invaluable life lesson this experience gave me. It highlighted the true essence of what matters most in my life.

But the story doesn't end there. Let's journey ahead to 2020, where, despite finding fulfillment in my chosen field, a sense of longing began to creep in once more. It is a sentiment that often accompanies those of us who possess a restless spirit, constantly seeking new horizons, fresh challenges, and the next exhilarating endeavor.

Instead of grappling with it by myself, I made a decision that would shape my life—I hired my very own therapist/life coach to help me bring more purpose and joy into my life. This wasn't just any coach. She was also a yoga teacher, and an incredibly accomplished one at that—someone who viewed life through a similar lens. It was during this transformative period that my coach introduced me to the concept of composing a dharma statement (also known as a life purpose statement), something I had never heard of before.

This moment was a spiritually integrated one for me. It proved to be extremely pivotal, a true aha moment that brought clarity to my ultimate purpose and how to deliver it. With her guidance, I carefully crafted my dharma statement. It was the first time I had articulated my purpose in such concrete words. It came from a place deep in my spirit and not from my head, and that was the magic I was missing! I wrote it down, printed it out, and enthusiastically shared it with those around me. With their support and enthusiasm, my dharma statement gained even more traction and generated increased enthusiasm. This transformative experience propelled my understanding of my personal dharma to even greater depths, influencing the very essence of how I "show up" and engage with life itself. (You can look forward to learning more about dharma and purpose in chapter 6.)

This was yet another catalyst on my personal journey that brought me closer to my calling. Just like any other facet of existence, this journey of mine is an ever-evolving one, grow-ing and transforming alongside my own personal development (just like yours is). It is now MY personal mission to share this invaluable tool of achieving purpose with others, empowering people like you to unlock their fullest potential in life and get clear on what they are here to achieve.

With a résumé that includes career development roles in non-profit, college, and large corporation settings, a master's degree in counseling, HR and recruitment experience, and over 10 years as a yoga teacher, I approach the world of career and purpose coaching from a truly holistic perspective. It is my sincere ambition that this perspective serves as a transformative gateway for you, leading you towards breakthroughs in discovering who you are and what you are here to do.

WHAT IS THE PURPOSE FORWARD SYSTEM, AND HOW IS IT DIFFERENT FROM OTHER CAREER EXPLORATION METHODS?

The book you are holding in your hands is the exact system I use in my career & life purpose coaching practice. It is a complete system born from many arduous hours of experience working with clients and students to demystify the self-discovery process and the path to personal fulfillment. The methods presented here have been honed and refined through comprehensive work in my coaching practice with fellow Purpose Seekers who, like you, have sought guidance to help them uncover deeper meaning in their lives and careers. Purpose Forward was developed as an answer for individuals who have felt stuck or disappointed and are seeing a lack of results with traditional methods.

And it works!! Individuals who sincerely put effort into this program really do get results.

The Purpose Forward System is an integrative method that pulls on techniques from various modalities, including career & purpose coaching; acceptance and commitment therapy (ACT); strength-based, mindfulness-based coaching; yoga psychology; and positive psychology. It begins with taking a deep dive into your own unique nature, including your personality, conditioning, and self-esteem. It helps you to reflect on your passions, values, and strengths, which serve as a GPS that points you in the direction of your purpose.

From there, we take a holistic inventory of the physical, cognitive, emotional, and spiritual elements of self-care, which I see as making up the foundation of meaningful change. Then we plunge into understanding your life narrative and how your very personal life story is continuing to evolve. You learn what dharma is, how it works, and how to uncover your own unique blueprint.

You will "graduate" this book with:

- ✓ A life purpose (dharma) statement
- ✓ A personal mission statement
- ✓ An inspired list of realistic career (and passion) options
- ✓ A targeted résumé plan
- ✓ An impactful cover letter plan
- ✓ A job search strategy
- ✓ A personal branding kit for networking and interviewing

You will be guided in setting both the happening-soon and happening-later goals, empowering you to overcome any wavering self-confidence. Most importantly, Purpose Forward charts a clear path from not having any clue what you want to do to finding your purpose, all while keeping you motivated and resilient throughout!

HOW TO USE THIS BOOK

This is the kind of book you can push through in a day or thoughtfully savor for months. Go at the pace that feels most comfortable and meaningful to you. It is not a race, and to be honest, you will most likely see the best results if you take the time to digest it and put full effort into the provided exercises.

Throughout each section, you will find powerful reflection questions designed to get you thinking (and feeling!) about important concepts. (Jot down your answers or simply think through them if you prefer.) Think of these concepts as "keys" that will ultimately help you unlock your purpose. These questions are really the core of the book and are what will ultimately open the door to the insight and awareness that the pursuit of purpose requires.

If writing out the answers feels too academic and you are not feeling it, do not stress! Do it in your head. Draw it out instead. Tell the answer to your dog. Or just skip it altogether! Find a process that will support you and make this an enjoyable experience! You can't do this wrong.

There are infinite selections of intelligent resources to assist you as you explore your next steps forward—your high school or college career center, mentors, parents, friends, podcasts, social media posts, and many other books. You can spend a significant amount of time going through it all.

It is extremely overwhelming, I know!

This book was created to give you a solid, go-to, no-nonsense resource to actually make it happen. Because time is valuable, and I have your back! I crafted this book to answer the very needs I once had. It is intended to bring you immense benefit and personal growth, just as it has for myself and the many clients I've worked with directly.

Finally, this book is about setting an intention, taking action, and seeing results. Commit to this process, and by the time you finish this book, you will undoubtedly understand the nature of your calling.

So go ahead. We start this journey together, right now. Get your pen and get comfortable; here we go!

Think about what your intention is in doing this work and what made you open this book. You want to declare it in the present tense as if it has already manifested. This may feel strange, but trust me, it's important. Writing in the present tense is how we truly embody the message.

Here are some examples of what this might look like:

"I am living a life of purpose."

"I have a purposeful career."

"I discovered the ultimate strengths I needed to bring to my current role."

"I have brought more of my passions into my everyday life."

"I am clear on the next steps needed for my job search."

"I am confident in my purpose and able to share my dharma statement with others."

Ok, your turn. Give it a shot. My intention is...

_____

_____

_____

_____

Fabulous job! See, that wasn't so hard! Your journey to unleashing insights that will lead you straight to a life bursting with joy and purpose begins—now!

May you be blessed with the wisdom to know who you are.

To spread your light and manifest your desires.

May you live from a place of creativity and curiosity

and dive deeper to understand the essence of who you truly are.

Where you have been and where you are headed.

Now that we've got all of that out of the way, it's on to the first chapter, where we can explore a bit about who you are!

STEP 1

EXPLORING: WHO AM I?

CHAPTER 1

WHAT IS PURPOSE?

"I honor the divinity within myself. I discover and embrace my true nature and I allow my life work to be, being myself."

—Sheri Mabry

Our Purpose. Our Dharma. Our Duty. Our Calling. Our Spark. Our Life's Work. Our Essential Nature. Our Contract. Our Mission. Choose the phrase that most resonates with you. Go ahead and put a little heart around the one that speaks to you. ☺

It's something we are supposed to know. It is by igniting that "spark" within us that we are reminded why we are here on this earth, in this particular moment in time, with these particular people around us.

And it's ultimately just being ourselves. Sounds simple, right?

But being ourselves on purpose.

A meaningful life will look very different for you than it will for your neighbor. It's a personal journey as unique as the rhythm in your favorite song, tailor-made to speak directly to your soul. The kind that makes you bop your head back and forth with joy and ease. A unique song that evolves with you as you transition through different seasons of life. One that takes into account your passions, values, strengths, and the ultimate story your life is telling. (You are thinking about your life story right now, aren't you? Don't worry, we will get deeper into that a few chapters in!)

I like to think of our purpose as a "contract" we make with ourselves before we even take form in this life. The *ultimate* contract will remain intact—it is like the title of a book. The chapters will transition through the various twists and turns your life will naturally take, but they all plug into the book title—your ultimate purpose.

We are going to get there together over the course of this book. You will soon have your own guiding statement to help you navigate through the chapters of your personal story. Stay with me, Purpose Seeker!

WHY DO WE NEED PURPOSE?

Living out your dharma (life purpose) allows you to be part of a cause greater than yourself—it allows you to serve others and honor your essential nature. It will "activate" your life, bring your soul into harmony, and I bet it will make you feel pretty darn good about yourself too. Living your purpose gives your brief days on this earth a much richer meaning and a genuine sense of fulfillment. Being in tune with your life purpose is like having your own private compass that will remind you of where you should direct your attention—and highlight your most treasured priorities in your life.

HOW DO WE ACCESS PURPOSE?

You may have learned about this in Intro to Psychology. You know, that mandatory class you had to take when you thought you wanted to be a psych major ☺. Let me give you a super-quick refresher. Maslow's Hierarchy of Needs is a theory proposed by the psychologist Abraham Maslow to explain human motivation and the progression of human needs. The hierarchy is often shown as a pyramid with five levels, with the most basic physiological needs at the bottom and the highest-level psychological needs at the top.

We can't fully appreciate the pathway to achieving purpose without an understanding of this hierarchy. Achieving purpose is a component of self-actualization, which is right at the top of the pyramid.

In order to reach the top (self-actualization), we need to have our basic needs met first—like food, shelter, and safety. (Can we add our cell phone to this list yet?!)

Following basic needs, self-confidence grows from our relationships with others and having a sense of belonging. Once we can firmly stand in our own esteem and feel self-actualized, we can begin to think about purpose.

Let's just say you are fortunate enough to live a life of purpose—

With access to the right resources, mentors, and training—with enough grit, skillful intention, and concrete action—we are all capable of reaching our fullest potential. And that will look remarkably unique for each one of us because we all hold a deeply specialized set of life experiences, strengths, and passions.

You may have already put in a great deal of effort to discover your purpose. Over the years, you've probably sought advice from parents, friends, teachers, your rabbi, the Uber driver, and wise Uncle Al. Perhaps you've taken self-assessments, sought resources, or even worked with a career coach. Maybe, despite crafting your questions perfectly, even ChatGPT wasn't able to give you all the answers you desired. Many of these tools are very valid and helpful. But if they *still* aren't getting you results, you need to look deeper.

First, you need to understand the truest core of who you are as a unique human being. Sounds simple, right? But we know this is not easy.

It is actually some of the deepest work we will do in this life.

> *Once you find yourself, you will simultaneously uncover your purpose.*

Once you embrace your purpose, you can live in alignment with your personal truth. This is how we reach our fullest potential.

What Purpose Is *Not*

Let's get one thing clear: Purpose is not *necessarily* your job or career. Purpose is all the things we do and experience that bring our awareness to the present moment in a way that manifests gratitude. It's what brings us joy, meaning, and fulfillment. It's when we are tapping into our unique creativity and are in "flow." It is what happens within when we are doing this "work." Put simply, you find yourself by doing what you love.

Can you live your purpose through your career? Absolutely! Is it necessary? Nope!

Purpose is not what you do. It's how you show up.

It is through the ordinary of every day that we live our purpose. (By the way, go watch the Disney movie *Soul* if you have not already. It does a brilliant job of explaining this point.) It's the light you share with others by just being yourself. Every one of us has a purpose. We are all unique and beautiful.

You can use this book to simply discover your purpose and NOT plug it into a career. Or you can. ☺

The choice is yours.

Sometimes our job doesn't fulfill our purpose, and that is OK. But for the scope of this book, we will investigate how you can align your purpose with a career if you choose to. I will also introduce you to other possibilities.

PURPOSE AND LONGEVITY

Have you heard of "blue zones" before?

"Blue zones" are small regions around the world where residents have a significantly higher than average life expectancy, with many living to be 100 years old or older! There are many theories as to what factors contribute to this longevity. But there's one very interesting thing many of them have in common: A sense of purpose is often a key component of their lifestyles. Here are a few worth noting:

Okinawa, Japan: Okinawans use the term "ikigai," which roughly translates to "a sense of purpose" or "reason for being."

Sardinia, Italy: In Sardinia, a devotion to community and family plays a significant role, providing them with a strong sense of purpose and connection.

Nicoya Peninsula, Costa Rica: People in Nicoya have a term called "plan de vida," which means "soul's purpose." It's often translated as "why I wake up in the morning." They have a strong sense of community and focus on healthy and active life-styles, which also contribute to a sense of purpose and well-being.

Ikaria, Greece: The residents here have a strong sense of community and a slower pace of life. This offers them a sense of purpose and deep contentment.

Many of the people in these blue zones maintain a clear sense of purpose throughout their entire lives, even well into old age. You can frequently find them doing things that bring them joy and fulfillment, including tending their gardens, creating art, danc-ing, singing, or mentoring their families. This sense of purpose keeps them mentally and emotionally engaged in their community, contributing to their overall well-being, and ultimately assisting them in having a very long and happy life!

These observations serve as affirmation that the em-phasis on purpose serves as a motivator for living a long and fulfilling life. And I know this is some-thing you want in your life too!

PURPOSE CANNOT BE FOUND
THROUGH INTELLECT ALONE

I find myself chuckling whenever students or clients get super "heady" with finding their purpose. You see, the thinking mind is useful for certain specific things, like doing your taxes, reading maps, or following along with the ingredients in a recipe. But purpose can't be arrived at through intellect alone, my friend.

In fact, it is pretty much the exact opposite.

> *Purpose is a feeling-mind concept, not a thinking-mind concept. It is like dancing, writing a poem, or sketching out a drawing. Therefore, it can only be found through the feeling-mind process.*

My intention for this book is to help you arrive at your dharma by feeling your way to it.

Don't worry if you are a thinker. I promise we will use our left-side, logical brains too!

CHAPTER 2

MY NATURE/NURTURE

The opening to this chapter became clear as I read my daughters their bedtime story from the classic The Velveteen Rabbit, *because everything we need to know we learn by kindergarten, right?!*

"Real isn't how you are made," said the Skin Horse. "It's a thing that happens to you. When a child loves you for a long, long time, not just to play with, but REALLY loves you, then you become Real."

"Does it hurt?" asked the Rabbit.

"Sometimes," said the Skin Horse, for he was always truthful. "When you are Real you don't mind being hurt."

"Does it happen all at once, like being wound up," he asked, "or bit by bit?"

"It doesn't happen all at once," said the Skin Horse. "You become. It takes a long time. That's why it doesn't happen often to people who break easily, or have sharp edges, or who have to be carefully kept. Generally, by the time you are Real, most of your hair has been loved off, and your eyes drop out and you get loose in the joints and very shabby. But these things don't matter at all,

because once you are Real you can't be ugly, except to people who don't understand."

—Margery Williams Bianco

We begin our purpose-discovery journey by first understanding who we are. This passage from the classic story *The Velveteen Rabbit* says it all. Our authenticity, our very essence, blossoms when embraced by love. And sometimes, unfortunately, in real life—we do not get all of the love we need from others. (Less than perfect parents? They are out there, and that's OK!)

In those moments, the responsibility falls upon us to cultivate our own self-love, for it is in this act of self-nurturing that we emerge truly "Real." We can only do it for ourselves.

When we learn to love ourselves deeply, not just superficially, we undergo a transformation. It's a process that happens over time. It's through the process of self-love that we shed the masks we may have worn to please others or fit societal expectations. We allow our authentic selves to emerge, unapologetically. It can be a vulnerable and sometimes painful journey, but when we truly love and accept ourselves, we are one step closer to knowing our unique purpose.

As the story explains, becoming "Real" doesn't happen all at once. It's a gradual unfolding of our true essence. We let go of the need for perfection and embrace our imperfections and vulnerabilities. And that is a very beautiful thing! The love we cultivate for ourselves sustains us through the challenges we face, making us resilient to any disappointments that may come our way.

I know, I know—trying to find yourself amidst the chaos of college is like trying to find a shooting star on a cloudy night on your weekend trip to New York City! Between 30-page papers, 2 a.m. study sessions, and the perpetual quest for caffeine, it's no wonder self-discovery is on the back burner. You've had more syllabi to read than you've had moments to ponder the meaning of life!

Just when you think you've found a moment of long-awaited peace, your roommate bursts into the room with the latest relationship drama, or your professor decides to assign a last-minute group project. Who has time for deep contemplation when you're juggling exams, dating, part-time jobs, extracurriculars, and the occasional existential crisis?

But fear not, you'll stumble upon yourself in the most unexpected moments—perhaps in the laughter shared with friends over a fancy box of wine or in that delightful moment when the crush you've been stalking on social finally slides into your DMs. So, keep those eyes open, embrace the madness, and remember that even in the busiest of times, you're still on the path to discovering the amazing person you're becoming.

The transformation unfolds through doing the deep work of exploring our inner selves, exercising self-awareness by accepting our strengths and flaws, and truly owning what we find. It doesn't happen all at once—it is a process and a practice. There are no shortcuts. But this is where the journey begins, Purpose Seekers!

This is how the process needs to begin.

Those aha moments aside, perhaps we can only truly understand ourselves when we appreciate the intricate conversation of our genetics, environment, and upbringing. We need this cornerstone first—before we can plug it into our purpose.

So, what are nature and nurture exactly?

Here is something else you may remember from psych class (I'm so sorry, but I was a psych major and so much of this stuff is very fitting!):

Nature is the biological/genetic component of our various physical, cognitive, and emotional characteristics. This includes certain hereditary factors, such as temperament and predispositions, that can influence how we interact with the environment, as well as the development of certain personality traits. This is why some people may be naturally introverted or extroverted, open to new experiences, or like to plan ahead.

Nurture represents the environment's impact on the development of these traits. This includes the various forms of learning that take place through exposure to external factors such as family, neighborhood, culture, education, and life experiences. This can explain why we see correlations between things, such as why Black students who grow up with Black teachers are more likely to become teachers themselves or why individuals growing up in families that prioritize education are more likely to find academic success.

Who you are at your core represents some integration of your nature and your nurture—your genetics and your experiences. Pursuing the pathway of purposeful fulfillment requires an understanding of the uniqueness that is you. So, let's dig in a little deeper to uncover a fuller understanding of how you're wired and how this can help you align with your true calling.

PERSONALITY

*"I'm not shy. I'm holding back my awesome-
ness so it doesn't overwhelm you."*

—Anonymous

WHAT IS PERSONALITY?

Personality is defined as the unique set of enduring patterns of thoughts, feelings, and behaviors that characterize an individual and set them apart from others. These traits often correspond with our personal interests and preferences. For this reason, our personalities often dictate what career paths we find fulfilling. When we consciously align our career path with our personality traits, we are more likely to find careers that bring us contentment and gratification!

Our personality types are often indicators of our communication styles, work preferences, and overall strengths. Having this intel helps point us in the direction of career choices that resonate with our true selves.

When we are in careers that support our personalities, we tend to perform better and are more likely to excel in our roles!

There are numerous theories regarding personality and a number of different assessments available that can shed light on an individual's personality type. Below, we'll review two of the most common personality measures in career exploration.

Understanding personality is a fundamental aspect of the Purpose Forward program. Gaining insight into your personality is a critical first step in finding the career path that best suits you. In fact, I always have my clients share their personality type with me prior to our first session, as it directly impacts how I connect with and empower them.

MBTI ASSESSMENT

And now it is my distinct pleasure to introduce you to my personal favorite personality assessment, the Myers-Briggs Type Indicator (most commonly known as the MBTI). I fell in love with it the first day I learned about it. I took an in-depth course that stimulated me so much that I was literally dreaming about it every night for two months! To this day, I love trying to guess people's MBTI types, and I have to say I'm pretty good at it. You could say it's one of my personal superpowers ☺.

The MBTI is one of the most well-known and widely used self-report personality assessments. It was developed by Katharine Cook Briggs and her daughter, Isabel Briggs Myers, based on the personality theories proposed by Carl Jung. It has been popular for several decades and is commonly used in various settings, including workplaces, high schools and colleges, and self-development programs. It is a trusted tool for exploring the relationship between personality types and careers.

The assessment categorizes individuals into one of sixteen personality types based on their preferences across four dichotomous pairs of personality traits:

- Extraversion (E) or Introversion (I)

- Sensing (S) or Intuition (N)

- Thinking (T) or Feeling (F)

- Judging (J) or Perceiving (P)

Each personality type is represented by a four-letter code, such as INFP or ESTJ.

Each MBTI personality type is associated with its own characteristic career preferences, relational styles, wellness attitudes, and general psychological makeup. The MBTI produces results that can guide you towards professions that resonate with your strengths and passions, ultimately leading to a more fulfilling and purposeful career. The connection between MBTI types and careers has been established through a combination of qualitative and quantitative research, including surveys, case studies, and observations of individuals in various occupations. Researchers and practitioners have established recurring themes and tendencies in the preferences and strengths of individuals with specific MBTI types in certain career fields.

Connect to the resources page to take the official "MBTI Instrument" personality type assessment.
https://tinyurl.com/purposeforwardresources

It is fee-based, but it includes a write-up of your type and everything you will need to know about it. There's also a free online version of this assessment if you prefer.

Here is a super-quick version. Go ahead and circle the example you tend to gravitate towards in each pairing:

MYERS–BRIGGS TYPE INDICATOR (MBTI)

Q1. Extraverted (E) vs. Introverted (I)

Which is your most natural energy orientation?

Extraverted Characteristics	Introverted Characteristics
I act first, then think/reflect later	I think/reflect first, then act

Q2. Sensing (S) vs. Intuition (N)

Which way of understanding is most natural to you?

Sensing Characteristics	Intuitive Characteristics
I trust what is certain/concrete	I trust inspiration

Q3. Thinking (T) vs. Feeling (F)

How do you like to make decisions?

Thinking Characteristics	Feeling Characteristics
Based on facts and logic	I instinctively employ personal feelings and impact on people

Q4. Judging (J) vs. Perceiving (P)

How do you structure your life?

Judging Characteristics	Perceiving Characteristics
I like knowing what I am getting into and making plans ahead of time	I'm comfortable moving into action without a plan; I plan on the go

Now write down the letter that corresponds to each dichotomy that represents your personality. It will look something like ISTJ, ENFP, INFJ

MY MBTI type is:

Now that you know your type, you can have an absolute field day learning more about your personality—strengths and weaknesses, how you show up in relationships as a supervisor, etc. It can be freakishly like getting a horoscope reading! To explore this info, simply do a Google search for your type and see the associated common characteristics.

Here are a few highlights that stand out to me about my type:

_____

_____

_____

_____

_____

_____

You can learn about how your type corresponds to potential career paths. Google your type and career satisfaction—for example, try "Career for INFJ"—and find even more examples. Truity.com is a great resource for this.

These are the top five careers/fields that look interesting to me and that are associated with my MBTI type:

1. _____

2. _____

3. _____

4. _____

5. _____

We will revisit this list later in the book and learn ways to explore these potential options.

The book *Do What You Are* by Paul D. Tieger and Barbara Barron-Tieger is an excellent resource for looking further into what "careers" tend to be enjoyed by each type and, specifically, why.

THE HOLLAND CODE

Another top career assessment is called the Holland Code, also known as RIASEC. The Holland Code was developed by John L. Holland, an American psychologist, in the 1950s. This one breaks down personality into six different types:

Here is a brief description of each type:

Realistic (R): Prefer working with their hands and enjoy physical activities.

Investigative (I): Enjoy intellectual and analytical activities, focusing on problem-solving and research.

Artistic (A): Creative and expressive. Enjoy activities related to art, design, and self-expression.

Social (S): Have strong interpersonal skills, enjoy helping others, and thrive in social settings.

Enterprising (E): Enjoy leadership and entrepreneurial activities. Have high ambition and are persuasive.

Conventional (C): Enjoy structured and organized activities. Have attention to detail and like working with data and systems.

You can take a free assessment here to determine your type:
https://tinyurl.com/purposeforwardresources

Upon completion, your results will shed some light on your unique traits and values. You'll gain insights into potential career paths that align with your personality type while also discovering careers that may be best to steer clear of.

While many of us have one dominant type, looking at your three strongest types gives you the fullest understanding of your interests.

If you want to skip the formal version of this assessment, take a look at the descriptions listed above for each type. Put a number 1, 2, or 3 next to the ones that describe you most accurately. It will look something like SEA, CAE, RIA, etc.

My RIASEC Letters (in order):

_____

A few highlights that stand out to me about my RIASEC type:

_____

_____

_____

_____

My top five careers associated with this that look interesting to me:

1. _____

2. _____

3. _____

4. _____

5. _____

Looking at your results for both the MBTI and the RIASEC together will be very helpful in giving you a holistic picture of your personality. Again, we will revisit the career options associated with them later in the book.

WHY IS UNDERSTANDING PERSONALITY IMPORTANT?

Awareness of our personality can help us make sense of how we respond to and think about the world around us, and it can also help us understand our true essential nature.

For example, I have seen the aha moment that comes when a client discovers and accepts the fact they enjoy more time alone, dread being assigned a group project, and prefer communicating through writing (Introvert). I have also seen the joy someone experiences when they recognize they are happier in a job where they can actually be around people, love communicating often with many different individuals, and are actually energized by talking for hours! (Extrovert).

I see their eyes light up when they discover WHY they make decisions differently than the rest of their team. Perhaps they are more emotional, sensitive, and considerate of others' feelings (Feeler) when the rest of the group is looking at facts, data, and logic (Thinker).

When we understand who the heck we are, it is easier to understand the nature of the work and culture in which we will best flourish. When we can "own" our authentic selves, we no longer fear being hurt. We have the courage to be authentic and to show up as our true selves. We are not defined by external appearances or societal standards. Instead, we radiate a beauty and confidence that comes from within—that spark that can only be seen and appreciated by those who understand the depth of authenticity. And the right employer will definitely want to snatch that up!

"Be yourself; everyone else is already taken."

—Oscar Wilde

CONDITIONING

"Your own self-realization is the greatest service you can render the world."

—Ramana Maharshi

WHAT IS CONDITIONING?

FROM THE MOMENT WE LEAVE our mother's womb, we find ourselves swaddled in a patchwork quilt (from your loving grandma) of influences. Whether it's the nurturing (or not so nurturing) guidance of our parents, our cultural heritage, or society itself, we are constantly shaped by our surroundings. The neighborhood we are born into, the presence or absence of religious beliefs, our socioeconomic status, the company we keep, and the impact of teachers all leave their mark on us.

If you are like most people, even amidst all of these external influences, you probably still accept these beliefs as your own. But the truth is far more complicated.

This section aims to empower you to discover your own genuine belief system—not one that was given to you through osmosis. It will help you to unearth your most authentic self, transcending what you were simply handed and allowing you to embrace a truly personal and self-constructed worldview.

Let's get started!

ROLES

In life, we have many roles that define who we are and how we contribute to the world. We play different parts, like being a family member, friend, coworker, or citizen. These roles aren't fixed labels; they change and grow as we go through life. Embracing these roles helps us take on responsibilities, show who we are, and make a difference in the lives of others. Each role we play adds meaning to our story and connects us to the larger world around us.

Think of the roles you play in life. What do you default to when you think of who you are? (The Jerry Seinfeld of witty comebacks, the Taylor Swift of poetic creativity, or the Howie Mandel of cleanliness, perhaps?)

It may be your role in relationships, a career, a mindset, or a hobby.

For example, you may describe yourself as a son/partner/accounting intern/guitar player. Here are some exercises to get your wheels turning:

What comes to mind when I think of who I am? What roles do I play on the stage of life? For each role, write up a "job description" that describes the responsibilities and expectations it entails. For example, as a child of your parents, what roles do you have that fall under both spoken and unspoken agreements?

Now for each role—was there someone around me that I learned it from?

Role:

_____

Where I Learned It:

_____

_____

_____

_____

Am I happy with these roles, or are there any I would like to kick to the curb, like yesterday's blog post? Do my roles serve the highest good for myself, the others, and the whole of the relationship? Why?

_____

_____

_____

_____

Who would I be if the role disappeared or was adjusted? And would it affect anyone else to let it go and tweak my "job description"? What would that look like?

_____

_____

_____

_____

ARCHETYPES

Now go a bit deeper. Let's talk about archetypes for a moment. An archetype is like a well-known character that everyone easily understands because it stands for a particular idea or feeling. Just think about heroes in stories or movies—they're like the brave people we all look up to. Archetypes help storytellers and artists (like you!) share their messages in a way that everyone can connect with. Or, in this case, give you some terminology to describe some themes in your life.

What archetypes come to mind for you? Don't overthink it. Just think of different personas that describe you. Some common ones I hear:

- Helper
- Inspirer
- Mother
- Father
- Seeker
- Warrior
- Peacemaker

- Villain
- Child
- Advocate
- Intellectual
- Visionary
- Caregiver

Think about the ones that show up in the shows and movies you watch or in the books you read. The list goes on indefinitely!

Here are some more examples:

Archetypes
Mentor: A wise and guiding figure that imparts knowledge and helps the protagonist on their journey.
Lover: Represents themes of passion and romance.

Rebel: A character who challenges norms and authority, sparking change and revolution.
Explorer: Reflects a deep desire for discovery and adventure, often seen in tales of exploration and quests for the unknown.
Joker or Trickster: A mischievous character that brings humor and unpredictability.
Sage: A wise and insightful character who provides guidance through their knowledge and experience.

Which ones do I have qualities of? What others can I add to this list?

_____

_____

_____

_____

_____

Now let's talk about the person or people who raised you (usually a parent or guardian).

What beliefs about work and career did I receive (or not receive) from my family during my childhood? What did they teach me (or not teach me?)

_____

_____

_____

_____

_____

Did my parents or guardians have specific expectations or aspirations for my career path? How did that influence my own beliefs about what defines a "successful" career?

_____

_____

_____

_____

_____

Were there any specific experiences or events during my childhood that ignited my passion for a particular field or area of interest?

_____

_____

_____

_____

_____

What are the things I admire about my caretakers and the things I don't want to duplicate? What are their beliefs and values? These may be political, financial, or religious views, passions, or just a general outlook on life. Of course, this can be a heavy or uncomfortable topic to consider, and a deep analysis of your upbringing may be beyond the scope of this book. That said, I encourage you to take a moment to reflect on it in an honest way and see what comes up for you.

Fill in this chart:

Person	Admire	Rather Not Duplicate	Beliefs/Values/Fears
Example: Mom	Zest for life Ability to build relationships Creativity with painting Family traditions	Works long hours Anxious Condescending at times	Strong religious values Stay positive always Always tries to save money Afraid of losing job Values diversity Family-focused

Person	Admire	Rather Not Duplicate	Beliefs/Values/Fears

Melissa M. Carvalho, M.A., RYT

Person	Admire	Rather Not Duplicate	Beliefs/Values/Fears

Person	Admire	Rather Not Duplicate	Beliefs/Values/Fears

Melissa M. Carvalho, M.A., RYT

Person	Admire	Rather Not Duplicate	Beliefs/Values/Fears

Now circle the ones that you have in you as well—from both the "admire" and "rather not duplicate" columns.

Any surprises there?

_____

_____

_____

_____

_____

Now let's talk about you.

What are my best qualities? (Go ahead; now is your chance! ☺)

_____

_____

_____

_____

_____

What are some things that I would like to change or improve about myself?

_____

_____

_____

_____

_____

_____

What fears do I have (rational or irrational)?

_____

_____

_____

_____

_____

_____

What life lessons were/are my caregivers here to learn? What was/is their life purpose or mission?

_____

_____

_____

_____

_____

Am I drawn to what they are, or something different? What am _I_ here to learn? What may my life purpose or mission be? (Don't worry; we will get much deeper into this, but if you have any hunches, put them down here.)

_____

_____

_____

_____

_____

WHY UNDERSTANDING CONDITIONING IS IMPORTANT

By taking some time to ponder our upbringing, we unlock a better understanding of how our sense of self came to be molded. Reflection helps us to understand the origins of this web of influences that has helped to shape our cherished values, steadfast beliefs, and expectations in life.

I have been amazed by the clarity and epiphanies that have come from doing this work with clients. It is incredible how an individual can move forward and stand confidently in their own truth once they uncover all of the ways their set of beliefs and their moral code were just handed to them.

This work is important.

Even if it can be hard to look at.

I once asked a client, "Are there any strong beliefs that your parents have? Have they steered you towards a specific path in life or certain way to live?" With genuine contemplation, he thought about this question, but nothing surfaced immediately. A week later, in the next session, he announced that he remembered that his parents raised him with the strong intention of him becoming a priest! I literally lol'd. I think that may be the ultimate example of hidden parental expectations!

The act of objectively examining our upbringing and conditioning from a detached vantage point holds transformative power. It allows us to perceive any interferences or limits we might have unknowingly absorbed. It liberates us! And we can move forward with a bright new clarity and the capacity to make optimal decisions for our own lives.

Our conditioning intricately converses with the realm of self-imposed limitations and our self-perception, both of which we will delve into next!

SELF-ESTEEM

"Self-confidence is like a Wi-Fi signal—the stronger it is, the better the connection to success!"

—Author unknown

WHAT IS SELF-ESTEEM?

CLOSE YOUR EYES FOR A moment and ask yourself about moments when you exude self-esteem.

Go ahead.

I'll wait.

What do you see?

What are you doing, and how are you showing up?

Maybe it's the day you decide to wear a bikini at the beach, ask that love interest out on a date, speak up in front of the class, or express yourself creatively. To put it frankly, it's how you feel about yourself, even when no one is looking. Your self-image can be influenced by a multitude of things, including how you were raised, your cultural background, social interactions, experiences, and (gasp!) the media.

When it's positive, it's showing up as your true self and knowing your self-worth. A positive self-image creates resilience, allowing yourself to bounce back from bad experiences (who doesn't have those, right?!) and embrace personal growth. When it's negative, it's doubting your self-worth and feeling self-conscious or inadequate. It holds you back from reaching your full potential, limiting you from reaching your goals and being able to experience the genuine happiness of a life well lived.

So, how exactly do we obtain positive self-regard? It comes down to accepting yourself (who you are and who you are not), practicing self-care, surrounding yourself with positive influences, and challenging any negative self-talk.

Know that your self-esteem can change over time as you continue to evolve. It can be influenced by feedback you get from others, achievements you make, or significant life events. It plays a strong role in shaping your identity and influencing your responses to the events and circumstances that unfold around you.

If you have a hunch that enhancing your self-esteem could greatly benefit you, I strongly urge you to look into seeking the guidance of a therapist. It is a valuable step towards growth and it is well worth the investment! In the meantime, here are a few strategies that can help you scratch the surface.

A big shout-out to my clinical psychologist husband, who suggested a few more tips be added to this section, including techniques from cognitive behavioral therapy (CBT) and acceptance and commitment therapy (ACT). Being married to a psychologist definitely comes in handy (not to mention a lifetime of free therapy!)

Embrace and emphasize your strengths instead of fixating on your weaknesses.

When reflecting on my own strengths, these come to mind:

_____

_____

_____

_____

_____

_____

Here are the qualities that make me unique and awesome:

_____

_____

_____

_____

_____

_____

Now it's time to cultivate a positive mindset by recognizing your achievements and capabilities.

Here are a few of my favorite accomplishments: (Don't be shy!)

_____

_____

_____

_____

_____

_____

It's time for some action!

Think of some small challenges or behaviors you can introduce to help develop more confidence. For example, if you struggle with being timid, you could focus on developing stronger eye contact when engaging with others, or you could take the initiative to approach someone you don't know personally and ask for some career advice.

If you need more self-assurance regarding your skills, you can look to acquire new competencies through taking an online course, attending a workshop, or reading a related book.

Maybe you can gain confidence through developing a hobby such as playing the drums (my brother benefited from this dramatically as a kid!), gardening, sewing, or exercising (tell me you are not more confident when you bench-press!). When we develop mastery of a skill through repetition, we can feel pretty awesome about ourselves!

Here are some action steps I can take in my life to enhance my confidence:

_____

_____

_____

_____

_____

_____

Remember, building confidence doesn't happen overnight, so be patient and celebrate even the smallest victories along the way!

If you're having difficulty coming up with some strengths, fret not! We will explore this more deeply in the next chapter. By capitalizing on your strengths, acknowledging your accomplishments, and taking some small action steps, you will be well on your way to bolstering your self-esteem and getting the job (and life) you deserve!

LIMITING BELIEFS

Ah, the journey of starting your career! As you step into this adventure, you might come across something sneaky, which I'll refer to as "limiting beliefs." Imagine them as pesky little gremlins hiding in the corners of your mind, whispering doubts and fears about what you can achieve. But fear not, Purpose Seeker! Unraveling these limiting beliefs is like going on an epic quest to unleash your full potential and rock your career like a boss.

If I'm being honest, this section is my least favorite one to write because talking about negative things is not something I find especially enjoyable. I would much rather talk about purpose, joy, and things that light us up, but it's too important to leave out. I have seen unbelievable results come from these exercises.

If you are one of the few blessed souls fortunate enough to not entertain limiting beliefs about yourself, please feel free to skip this section and move onto something much more fun—passions! But if you are like most people and from time-to-time have negative thoughts or beliefs about yourself that hinder your personal growth and limit your potential, keep reading, my friend!

Limiting beliefs can arise from a number of different sources. They can be reflective of a distorted or negative self-esteem from within ourselves, or they can develop from the influence and messages of the people around us. They can be handed down intergenerationally through our families or influenced by society as a whole (think peers, media, social media, advertising, etc.). They can be about different parts of your life, maybe even your career.

They are thoughts such as these:

- "I'm not good enough."

- "I'm not qualified enough."

- "I'm afraid to take the risk."

- "I'll never find a job I love."

It can come from a fear of failure or being rejected. These thoughts sadly create self-imposed barriers, causing us to doubt our abilities and avoid taking risks, preventing us from pursuing opportunities or even getting started.

Here are some other common examples I hear from folks:

- "I can't work in that field."

- "I'm not good at math."

- "I'm too young/old for that career."

- "I don't have the right education to reach my dreams."

- "I don't have enough work experience to get the job I want."

It may also be that you can't be your real self, you self-sabotage, or you are a perfectionist. Perhaps you don't feel safe, or you feel unworthy or broken. Maybe you are healing from being let go at a job or a breakup. Maybe you "play small" and don't go for a better role because your lack of self-confidence is holding you back.

What are some limiting beliefs I have about myself that may be blocking me from getting the career I want? (Dig deep. Be honest here!)

_____

_____

_____

_____

Limiting beliefs can seep into all areas of our lives, like an infectious disease—into our relationships, finances, or health and wellness. Really, a limiting belief is one that holds you back and keeps you from being aligned with your true self.

What are some limiting beliefs I have about myself that may be blocking me from fulfillment in other areas of my life?

_____

_____

_____

_____

_____

Which of these phrases have been ingrained in me through conditioning? Where did the idea originate from?

_____

_____

_____

_____

_____

Do I recognize any fears that have arisen as a result? How have they restricted my potential?

_____

_____

_____

_____

Now let's dig in a bit.

Are these beliefs actually true? Can I legitimately claim absolute knowledge of their validity?

_____

_____

_____

_____

What evidence do I have to contradict them?

_____

_____

_____

_____

Here's a powerful one: Does the limiting belief serve me and my highest good?

_____

_____

_____

_____

If I let go of the thought, who would I become? What positive belief could I put in its place?

_____

_____

_____

_____

It all comes down to knowing that you are worthy. If it makes you feel better, ask others around you what you are good at—this can be friends, family, coworkers, neighbors, or partners. Build up your confidence and see things from a fresh perspective.

Maybe come up with a mantra that will serve you. Something like "I am worthy of a fulfilling career." "I am ready to take the next step." Or "I have the skills to do this job."

_____

"Self-awareness without judgement is the biggest spiritual practice"

—Swami Kripalu

_____

OK, it's time!!

Time to own your impact!

To step into your power!!

To go beyond the prison of your own limiting beliefs and unlock your full potential.

The world needs you!

Now that you have a bit more self-awareness, it will serve you well. Knowing who you are is the foundation of authenticity. It will carry you through the next section (not to mention throughout your life!!), where we explore other aspects of your unique identity, including your passions, values, and strengths.

CHAPTER 3

MY COMPASS

"If you don't know where you are, a map won't help."

—Watts Humphrey

N OW THAT YOU HAVE EXPLORED a bit about your identity, it's time to take it to the next layer. I like to imagine our sense of purpose as being divided into layers. Picture an avocado (it is a superfood after all, and you are pretty super!).

Your personality and conditioning are the core. It forms the unchanging foundation that shapes you.

The flesh of the fruit is your personal alignment and sense of purpose. This is made up of your passions, values, and strengths. When we are congruent with these, we will feel a deep sense of harmony.
This feeling of satisfaction leads to authenticity, fulfillment, and well-being. (This is the ultimate goal!!)

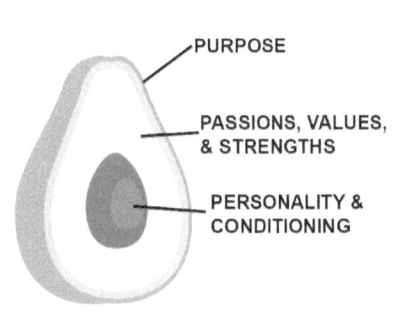

The external layer of the fruit represents the purpose we proudly display to the world. (More on that in chapter 6.)

Once we have these pieces, we will undoubtedly be much clearer about where we are headed.

Knowing who you are is your North Star. This will help direct your choices.

Let's start with passions. This is usually a fun topic for most of my clients.

PASSIONS

*"If you can't figure out your purpose, figure out your passion.
For your passion will lead you right into your purpose."*

—Bishop T. D. Jakes

WHAT ARE PASSIONS?

THIS QUOTE IS ABSOLUTELY SPOT-ON! Knowing and wholeheartedly embracing your passions is the quickest and easiest shortcut to getting to your purpose. It's definitely a good, strong hint in the right direction.

So, what is passion?

It is our interests.

The stuff we love to do.

The stuff that brings us deep fulfillment.

The activities that we can do endlessly and never get bored.

Our passions keep us engaged and continue to draw us in. They ignite a powerful spark within us—almost like an addiction—but a very healthy one, of course! ☺ They bring us a tremendous amount of joy and fulfillment… and we want more!

Unlike strengths, passions are not *necessarily* something we're good at doing, but we certainly want to continue to do it nonetheless!

Here are some prompts to help you begin to identify yours:

When am I in "flow" and just lose track of time—what am I doing? What could I do forever? Maybe there are one or two things that come to mind immediately. Maybe you even more! Go ahead and list the biggest ones here:

_____

_____

_____

_____

Isn't being in "flow" the best?!

Now, what lights me up and gives me a spark? What makes me come alive?

_____

_____

_____

_____

What would I do for free, if money were no object?

_____

_____

_____

_____

What would my life look like if I won 50 million dollars?

_____

_____

_____

_____

(Wasn't that an exciting one?!)

Now, think back to when you were a child (maybe 8–12 years old). What did you want to be when you grew up? Maybe it was a few different things. Put them all down. Even your superhero and famous athlete ones—because, you never know! Ask your parents if you need help jogging your memory.

_____

_____

_____

_____

What would I study if someone gave me a one-week paid vacation to learn or study one particular thing? What interests me and makes me want to learn more?

_____

_____

_____

_____

And here is the best question of all!

Are you ready?

Imagine you have five imaginary lives to lead. They don't even need to be realistic. What comes to mind?

Don't overthink this. Just write down the first things that pop into your head.

Here are some things I've heard:

- Living at the beach and having a hot dog stand

- Being an actor

- Traveling the world and making music

- Being a famous comedian while working on cars

You get the idea.

I have five imaginary lives. Go! And I'm not holding myself back!

_____

_____

_____

_____

_____

_____

_____

_____

_____

_____

_____

_____

_____

_____

_____

_____

_____

_____

_____

_____

_____

_____

_____

_____

_____

_____

_____

_____

_____

_____

_____

Wow, I love them.

How did that go for you? Hopefully that was fun!

Now look back at the lives... look closely. Is there one in particular that stands out—one that would make you squeal in delight?

Find it?

Good—highlight it, star it, tell your best friend about it!

Now, think about it for a hot second.

Is there any part of it that is realistic? Could there be a tiny sliver of wisdom in there that your higher self answered for you?

Are there any actionable steps you could take right now to explore that a bit more?

Now look back at your answers to the above questions. Do you notice any themes? What rises to the top regarding things that excite you?

_____

_____

_____

_____

_____

My top passions:

1. _____

2. _____

3. _____

"Don't ask yourself what the world needs. Ask yourself what makes you come alive. And then go do that. Because what the world needs is people who are alive"

—Howard Thurman

Now that you did some of that work on your own (we get much more accuracy when we come up with them organically and not necessarily when we are just handed a list), here are a few examples of passions that you may have.

Notice which ones in the list below resonate the most with you:

PASSION EXAMPLES

1. **Helping Others**—volunteering, social causes for both humans and/or animals, social work, healthcare, caregiving, teaching, counseling, mentoring, advocating for social justice, or any activity that involves making a positive impact on people's lives.

2. **Arts and Creativity**—visual arts, music, dance, performing arts, writing, culinary arts, and other forms of creative expression.

3. **Entrepreneurship/Business**—developing products or services, starting and growing a business, strategic problem-solving, and exploring innovative ideas and solutions.

4. **Technology/Science**—working with technology, coding, robotics, artificial intelligence, computer science, conducting experiments or research, employing mathematics, engineering, or any field that involves

Melissa M. Carvalho, M.A., RYT

innovation and advancement or building and tinkering with gadgets.

5. **Sports/Fitness**—sports such as soccer, basketball, tennis, swimming, running, martial arts, fitness classes, personal training, rock climbing, extreme sports, or any other physical activity that you enjoy!

6. **Nature/Environment/Travel**—passion for environmental conservation, wildlife protection, sustainability practices, gardening, hiking, camping, or anything that allows you to appreciate the natural world, including travel and exploring different cultures.

7. **Personal Development and Self-Improvement**—practicing mindfulness, meditation, yoga, or engaging in personal growth, learning, or spiritual activities.

8. **Leisure**—reading, watching movies and TV, spending time with friends and family, massages, video games, long drives, shopping, leisurely walks.

Now look at your top passion list, which you just created a few pages back. Do they fit into any of the categories above?

_____

_____

_____

Go ahead and circle or highlight them. Feel free to add in your own more appropriate categories here as well:

_____

_____

_____

See which categories catch your eye. Think about bringing them into your life as new things you really enjoy! Anything stand out to you?

_____

_____

_____

_____

_____

You should be feeling a bit more confident in being able to verbalize your passions now. They are the interests that you feel deeply connected to—interests that provide you with a whole lot of joy!

Note that the list above is just a few examples. Passions can vary widely among different people based on their interests, talents, and life experiences. Yours may be very different and not even show up on that list!

Now that you have a solid understanding of your passions, are you ready to move on to discovering what your values are? Values are extremely important in making sure the work you do is meaningful and important to you.

Let's do it!

VALUES

*"Core values serve as a lighthouse when the fog of
life seems to leave you wandering in circles."*

—J. Loren Norris

WHAT ARE VALUES?

J UST AS YOUR PASSIONS KEEP you engaged, your core
values serve as a meaningful compass that will point you
towards what is truly important to you. They are the fundamental beliefs and principles that guide your actions.

When you take the time to reflect on your values, you gain
clarity on who you are on an even deeper level. Your values set
the foundation for making decisions, setting goals, and continuing to point you towards your ultimate purpose. And that
is why you are here!

By being able to articulate your values, you have the opportunity to hitch your wagon to a purpose beyond your individual
self and reach the like-minded community that shares the same
sentiments. It helps to amplify the impact of your purpose!

So here we go!

What social causes am I passionate about? What am I an advocate for? What would I fight for?

_____

_____

_____

_____

_____

_____

What keeps me up at night? (And I'm not talking about your dog who snores!)

_____

_____

_____

_____

_____

What problem do I want to solve, and how would I solve it? (Take your time with this one!)

_____

_____

_____

_____

_____

_____

Here are some thoughts on how I see the world, and how I would like it to be: (This is an insightful one!)

_____

_____

_____

_____

_____

What THREE qualities would I like to be remembered for? How would I want someone to describe me after an interaction with them (when showing up as my best self)?

_____

_____

_____

_____

_____

What legacy do I want to leave behind when I'm gone?

_____

_____

_____

_____

_____

What am I most grateful for in my life?

_____

_____

_____

_____

_____

_____

Now, list some of your pain points. These are things that get a negative emotional reaction out of you. Maybe it's traffic, conflict, ignorance, poor customer service, tech glitches, or a lack of work-life balance.

_____

_____

_____

_____

_____

_____

Now flip it. What does that emotion reveal about the core value it represents? For example, traffic teaches us patience and resilience by training us to adapt and remain calm in challenging situations. Frustration from traffic may reveal the core value of valuing time and efficiency in one's daily life. Or it may reflect a desire for control.

As a personal example, arguing and people raising their voices goes right through me. It gets my blood boiling. What it shows is that I really value harmony. It is no surprise that I enjoy teaching yoga—an environment to create a safe space of peace and harmony. What values do your "pain points" point towards?

_____

_____

_____

_____

_____

Here is a list of values that people commonly hold. Go ahead and circle about 10–12 that resonate with you the most. They are intentionally not in alphabetical order, so they show up in a more organic and natural way.

VALUES LIST

Peace	Positivity	Creativity	Humility
Mastery	Joy	Nature	Choice
Support	Mastery	Integrity	Tolerance
Clarity	Innovation	Spontaneity	Love
Wisdom	Gratitude	Autonomy	Compassion
Equality	Self-Respect	Curiosity	Serenity
Adventure	Pride	Wellness	Devotion
Security	Honesty	Respect	Responsibility
Relaxation	Service	Learning	Play
Truth	Patience	Harmony	Persistence

Friendship	Authenticity	Power	Competency
Ambition	Action	Grace	Personal Growth
Pleasure	Trust	Humor	Passion
Achievement	Health	Calmness	Loyalty
Diversity	Community	Education	Faith
Stability	Strength	Truth	Optimism
Family	Enthusiasm	Productivity	Kindness
Abundance	Beauty	Generosity	Balance
Cooperation	Contentment	Leadership	Openness
Empathy	Intelligence	Spirituality	Discipline

Go ahead and add any you have that are not listed here:

_____

_____

_____

_____

_____

Now see if you can take that list with the circles above and the section with any you've added in and narrow it down to your 3 top values. The ones you absolutely cannot live without!

My top values:

1. _____

2. _____

3. _____

You did it!

You may very well have a different but related set of values for different parts of your life—including career, relationships, fitness and health, self-development, or spirituality. Take some time to ponder how your values may shift in the different avenues of your life.

Use this space for any notes:

_____

_____

_____

_____

_____

_____

Now that you have done the work of listing your passions and values, it's time to move onto your strengths—the things you are really good at. This is a very good topic to aid in strengthening your confidence (if you need more!).

Are you still with me? Have your eyes rolled back into your head yet?

I've got you!

We're forging ahead… together!

STRENGTHS

"Everybody is a genius. But if you judge a fish by its ability to climb a tree, it will live its whole life believing that it is stupid."

—Albert Einstein

WHAT ARE STRENGTHS?

BEAR WITH ME ON THIS one. I know it can be hard to think about the things you are good at, because you don't want to come off as arrogant or cocky (good for you!). But I promise you that this is just for you, and no one needs to ever see it ☺.

So take a deep breath and get grounded. Feel your feet on the ground and your heart within your chest. Instead of thinking and doing, allow yourself to "be" and feel.

It's time to think about the skills, talents, and gifts you have to offer this world. I have yet to meet any being who does not have something to offer the world. So I know you do, too!

Let's begin.

What comes naturally to me that others find more challenging?

_____

_____

_____

_____

_____

_____

_____

What is my superpower? (Go ahead—when you look into the essence of who you are, what is the unique gift you are blessed with?)

_____

_____

_____

_____

_____

_____

What accomplishment am I really proud of? Describe the situation. What skills did you use, and what were the results?

_____

_____

_____

_____

_____

_____

If I had to give a TED Talk (or workshop to complete strangers) on the spot, what would the topic be? What topic do I know so well that I could put together in just 10 minutes flat?

Let's just say I pay you a million dollars to sweeten the deal! ☺

_____

_____

_____

_____

_____

What do others say my talents are? (Ask 3-5 people if you need to.)

_____

_____

_____

_____

_____

When I'm at my best, the exact thing I'm doing is...

_____

_____

_____

_____

_____

What skills do I have that excite me?

_____

_____

_____

_____

_____

_____

STRENGTHSFINDER ASSESSMENT

Now that you've had a chance to think about your skills a bit, I'd like to introduce you to a resource called the StrengthsFinder assessment, known as CliftonStrengths. You can purchase the book *StrengthsFinder 2.0* by Tom Rath, and included in that is a unique access code to take the legit assessment.

Or, if you'd like—here is a free online version to check out instead: https://tinyurl.com/purposeforwardresources

Gallup developed the CliftonStrengths psychometric assessment, which reveals your top 5 strengths from 34 themes. It also provides tips on how to effectively use them in your work.

Here is a short list of some of the most popular strengths and definitions from the StrengthsFinder:

MOST POPULAR STRENGTHS FROM THE

1. **Achiever:** You have a strong drive to get things done and accomplish goals. You have a high level of productivity and get satisfaction from completing tasks.

2. **Learner:** You have a thirst for knowledge and enjoy the process of acquiring new skills and understanding. You have natural curiosity and a love for continuous learning.

3. **Responsibility:** You take ownership of your commitments and obligations. You are reliable, dependable, and dedicated to fulfilling your responsibilities.

4. **Relator:** You excel in building and nurturing deep, meaningful relationships. You enjoy connecting with others on a personal level and creating a sense of trust and closeness.

5. **Maximizer:** You are focused on excellence and bringing out the best in yourself and others. You have a sharp eye for strengths and strive for continuous improvement.

6. **Strategic:** You possess a talent for seeing patterns, analyzing situations, and formulating effective plans. You excel in creating strategies and finding innovative solutions.

7. **Individualization:** You have a knack for recognizing and appreciating the unique qualities of others. You are skilled at developing unique approaches to meet individual needs.

8. **Activator:** You have a sense of urgency and drive to take action. You are a catalyst for change, and you can motivate others to move forward and make things happen.

9. **Communication:** You excel in expressing yourself verbally or through writing. You have a talent for conveying ideas, capturing attention, and engaging others in meaningful conversations.

Go ahead and take the online assessment if you would like (listed above).

My Top 5 Strengths from the StrengthsFinder:

1. _____

2. _____

3. _____

4. _____

5. _____

Your strengths can fall within four different quadrants, including...

Executing	Knowing how to make things happen
Influencing	Knowing how to take charge, speak up, and make sure your team is heard
Relationship Building	Building strong relationships that can hold a team together and make the team stronger
Strategic Thinking	Helping teams consider what could be. You absorb and analyze information that can inform better decisions.

Are there one or two of these quadrants that you seem to fall within? How can you capitalize more on these strengths?

_____

_____

_____

_____

Coming from higher education and career development, I can't conclude this chapter without mentioning the skills most employers seek. The National Association of Colleges and Employers conducted a survey on the top eight career readiness competencies employers seek. These are the current ones:

DESIRED CAREER COMPETENCIES
(FROM THE NATIONAL ASSOCIATION OF COLLEGE AND EMPLOYERS)

Career & Self Development: Proactively develop oneself and one's career through continual personal and professional learning, awareness of one's strengths and weaknesses, navigation of career opportunities, and networking to build relationships within and without one's organization.

Communication: Clearly and effectively exchange information, ideas, facts, and perspectives with persons inside and outside an organization.

Critical Thinking: Identify and respond to needs based on understanding situational context and logical analysis of relevant information.

Equity & Inclusion: Demonstrate the awareness, attitude, knowledge, and skills required to engage equitably and include people from different local and global cultures. Engage in anti-racist practices that actively challenge the systems, structures, and policies of racism.

Leadership: Recognize and capitalize on personal and team strengths to achieve organizational goals.

Professionalism: Knowing work environments differ significantly, understanding and demonstrating effective work habits, and acting in the interest of the larger community and workplace.

Teamwork: Build and maintain collaborative relationships to work effectively toward common goals while appreciating diverse viewpoints and shared responsibilities.

Technology: Understanding and leveraging technology ethically to enhance efficiencies, complete tasks, and accomplish goals.

If you feel you'd like to brush up on any of these skills, I invite you to do so, as they are the top skills employers are looking for as they interview candidates.

To learn more about these desired career competencies, go to the resources page: https://tinyurl.com/purposeforwardresources

Some of the skills on this list that I'd like to further develop to make myself more attractive to potential employers include:

_____

_____

_____

_____

_____

_____

There! That wasn't so painful, was it?!

Being in tune with your strengths and skills can help you have more confidence as you move closer to revealing your ultimate purpose. In combination with your passions and values, your strengths serve as a compass pointing in the direction of your dharma, or calling.

I'm sure you may be getting a bit more curious about what your life purpose is. We are getting closer…!

But first, we need to set the stage with something very important. Like building a house, to reach our fullest potential, we need to have a very solid foundation to build upon. I believe that foundation is working in a space of holistic wellness. We cannot move forward until we are operating from a centered place of wholeness and well-being.

And this arises from action, not just a state of mind.

(Enter yoga teacher mentality!)

Trust me on this one. You don't want to miss this next chapter. It's what sets this book apart from all the rest, and it will ultimately make the difference between knowing your purpose and not being sure of it.

Here we go, Purpose Seeker! You are fab!! And I have all the faith in the world in you.

STEP 2

FOUNDATION SETTING: SELF-CARE

CHAPTER 4

SELF-CARE 101

Purpose cannot be arrived at through intellect. It is found through intuition.

WHAT ON EARTH DOES SELF-CARE have to do with purpose?!

That would surely be my top question if I were the reader here.

Why do I need to honor self-care to help discover my purpose?

What comes to mind?

Go ahead; you can do it!

OK, so here's the deal.

We often wait until it's too late for "self-care."

As I learned from my meditation teacher, Jillian Pransky—life is like a filling bathtub, brimming with stress that inevitably pours in. To avoid being overwhelmed, we mustn't forget to open the drain before it overflows.

Self-care serves as the key to draining the tub.

We need to keep ahead of it.

It doesn't need to be anything fancy. Self-care can be taking a walk, reading a book, meditating, exercising, cuddling with your kitty cat, or facetiming a friend. It may be as simple as just stating your needs.

Self-care is the foundational step to finding your purpose, simply by being in a good, decent, or at least a not-so-bad place.

I have worked with clients who, sadly, had been struggling with their emotional well-being. I must be candid; working with them, while immensely rewarding, has been uniquely demanding, and achieving tangible results has not always been the case.

Because they weren't ready.

For various reasons, some individuals may not yet be fully prepared to embark on the career/purpose journey they need.

I'm not going to throw a truckload of data at you, but let me spill the beans: From oodles of experience, I've seen the magic happen! The real deal is this: Working with peeps who take care of themselves and who are in a decent mental, emotional, physical, and spiritual groove brings out the best results.

When you have the courage to take off your blinders and look at the holistic picture that is your life, perspective shifts, and transformation can happen.

And you deserve that!

This topic could literally be its own book.

But for now, here is my abridged take on wellness of mind, body, and spirit. Packaged for you in this one simple chapter, in hopes that it is enough for you to at least begin to reflect on the various parts that make you who you are in these different realms. May these insights pave the way for you to find where you belong and ultimately uncover your true purpose. Because I so want that for you! 💜

THE 4 CORE DOMAINS OF WELL-BEING

Physical	Basic needs, what you eat, how you move, finding rest and sleep, physical health, and finances
Cognitive	Resting your mind, gratitude, positivity, and cognitive stimulation
Emotional	Seeking emotional support, connecting with your community, and having relationships
Spiritual	Taking part in things that connect you with a higher power, whether through spirituality, religion, nature, or something else that nourishes you

There are four domains that make up well-being: physical, cognitive, emotional, and spiritual, as described above. I define wellness as balanced, purposeful, and consistent self-care in each of these domains. Sure, it can be challenging to check all of these boxes on a daily or even weekly basis. We are not looking for perfection here. But if you feel a little off-kilter, see if there is an area you have been neglecting or even yet to discover. Maybe, just maybe, it is the missing piece to get your groove back.

These domains ideally integrate with each other, like a well-synchronized machine. A deficiency in one may ripple into the others, causing a domino effect of imbalance. For example, feeling extreme sadness from being lonely and not having your emotional needs met may very well affect your physical or spiritual health. Having physical discomfort can dampen cognitive abilities and emotions.

Because our mind, body, emotions, and spirit are all interconnected at any given time.

Now, think of how these domains are reflected (and intersect) in different areas of your life:

8 LIFE AREAS

Relationships
Health
Career
Finances
Spirituality
Recreation
Community
Self-development

Are there any categories above that jump out right off the bat, that you do well, or need to do more of?

Take note here:

_____

_____

_____

_____

_____

_____

_____

As we explore a bit deeper into each of the 4 Core Domains of Well-Being, you will notice that there is one important thread that will carry through all four—and that is mindfulness.

You see, the practice of mindfulness is the secret ingredient to understanding your whole self. Mindfulness is all about paying really close attention to what's happening right now and accepting it fully. It's giving your thoughts and feelings your full focus, so you can better understand how you're feeling and why you're feeling that way.

It's like giving your consciousness front-row seats to the intricate dance between your thoughts and emotions. By inviting mindfulness into your daily life, you will have a greater level of self-awareness and cultivate a deeper connection to your inner world, which will in turn offer you the opportunity to navigate life's challenges with clarity and purpose.

Let me introduce you to a pretty cool term you can impress your friends with at the next get-together.

Svadhyaya.

Svadhyaya is a Sanskrit term from ancient Indian philosophy and spiritual practices in the yoga tradition. It is a combination of two Sanskrit words: "sva," meaning self, and "adhyaya," meaning study or investigation. Together, Svadhyaya translates to "self-study" or "self-inquiry."

In the context of yoga and spiritual development, Svadhyaya involves the process of introspection, self-reflection, and self-awareness. It encourages you to explore and understand your inner self, thoughts, emotions, and beliefs, as well as your connection to the world around you.

What is the shortcut to all of this, you ask?

Meditation ☺

Meditation is creating the space for your mind to take a break. It's when you sit or relax quietly, focus on your breath, and enjoy the moment by staying present. It helps you feel calm and gives your busy thoughts a chance to settle down.

And don't worry; I won't leave you hanging. As you'll see in the next section, I've included some mindfulness meditation exercises, one for each of the four domains, that I hope you'll consider trying and maybe even incorporating into your daily life.

Now, let's take a deeper dive into the 4 Core Domains of Well-Being.

Let's start with the physical domain. For many, this is the easiest domain to understand. Maybe, because, well, it's physical, which makes it a tangible concept to wrap your head around.

PHYSICAL

"Exercise? I thought you said extra fries!"

—Unknown

WHAT IS THE PHYSICAL DOMAIN?

I T MAKES SENSE TO BEGIN with the domain that is the most relatable and easiest concept to grasp.

The job hunt can be exhausting (physically and emotionally!) so this is an important one. The core of the physical domain is taking care of your physical body in terms of health, diet, sleep, physical activity, and even having a solid foundation of financial security (think basic needs).

This may sound overly obvious, but it's worth emphasizing that you are not going to be in the best condition to thrive (or even simply look for work) if you are malnourished, overtired, and don't have a roof over your head. Optimal physical wellness includes eating well, getting regular exercise, managing your energy, and having a suitable living environment.

Physical health can commonly be disrupted by various aspects of mental health, particularly stress, anxiety, and depression.

Chronic stress and anxiety can lead to physical symptoms:

- Headaches/migraines
- Muscle tension
- Chest pain
- Palpitations
- Digestive issues (e.g., stomachaches, diarrhea, or constipation)
- Sleep disturbances

Depression can be associated with physical symptoms:

- Chronic fatigue
- Unexplained aches and pains
- Changes in appetite and weight
- Decreased libido

Mental health has an impact on various medical issues. Here are some examples:

MEDICAL ISSUES IMPACTED BY MENTAL HEALTH

Psychosomatic Disorders: These are physical ailments you may have that have no clear medical cause and are believed to be linked to psychological stress. Examples include irritable bowel syndrome (IBS), fibromyalgia, tension headaches, and somatic symptom disorder.

Autoimmune Conditions: Psychological stress may contribute to the aggravation of certain autoimmune conditions you may have, such as rheumatoid arthritis, psoriasis, and inflammatory bowel diseases.

Cardiovascular Issues: Chronic stress and unresolved emotional trauma can contribute to high blood pressure, an increased heart rate, and a higher risk of heart disease.

Immune System Suppression: Prolonged stress and emotional distress can weaken the immune system, making individuals more susceptible to infections and illnesses.

Skin Disorders: Stress and anxiety can worsen skin conditions like acne, eczema, and psoriasis.
Insomnia: Emotional issues like anxiety and depression can lead to sleep disturbances and chronic insomnia.
Weight Fluctuations: Emotional eating patterns due to stress or emotional distress can lead to weight gain or loss.
Chronic Pain: Psychological factors, such as stress and emotional trauma, can exacerbate chronic pain conditions, making your experience more intense and debilitating.

Take note if there are any that you recognize in your own life.

I've had a tidbit to share with you another scientific insight I personally find fascinating. The vagus nerve.

The vagus nerve, also known as the tenth cranial nerve, is a critical part of the autonomic nervous system. It regulates some essential functions like your heart rate, breathing, digestion, mood and emotions, and stress response. It also serves as the communication pathway between the gut and the brain (ever wonder why your stomach hurts when you feel upset?!)

The vagus nerve serves as an example of how closely the mind and emotions are connected to the body's physical responses. It reveals the intricate relationship between the brain and our body's reactions.

Ever hear the phrase, "Trust your gut"?!

There is a lot of weight behind that phrase. When we learn to honor the sensory input we get from our body, the better we can emotionally regulate ourselves by reducing anxiety, improving our mood, and just responding better to stress.

Now we are going to jump into some reflection questions pertaining to the physical realm of your well-being. Know that these are just barely beginning to scratch the surface.

Just use this as a simple checklist of things to take inventory of and see if there could be any gaps.

What kind of environment, climate, and home do I need to thrive?

_____

_____

_____

_____

_____

_____

NOURISHMENT

What do I eat, and when do I eat? Do I eat several small meals a day or very large ones? (Eating smaller meals will help with digestion and energy.) What foods (or substances) should I avoid?

_____

_____

_____

_____

_____

SPOTLIGHT CLIENT

I recently worked with a client who was struggling to find meaning in her current role. While actively seeking a new job, she recognized the importance of making the most of her current situation. She confided in me that her unhappiness had led to changes in her eating habits and introduced some not-so-healthy choices.

Together, we devised a plan to establish healthier eating boundaries and have more balanced meals. This positive change has not only boosted her energy levels but also improved her overall perspective. She's now making the best of her current circumstances as she stays motivated to explore the new career opportunities that await her!

Am I eating in a balanced way? Think vegetables, fruit, protein, carbohydrates, and healthy fats.

(There are plenty of resources available, such as the Mediterranean Food Pyramid or the Balanced Plate.) It may even be helpful to keep a food diary of what you consume daily.

The goal is to notice what your patterns are.

Also, pay attention to your water intake. Are you getting close to the recommended 64 ounces? (Water is massively important for thinking clearly and having energy, by the way. And it is GREAT for your skin!)

EXERCISE/ENERGY/REST

Am I exercising regularly? Am I engaging in fitness in a well-rounded way (strength training, cardio, stretching)?

_____

_____

_____

_____

_____

If you are looking to exercise but are not sure how to get started, feel free to check out my yoga and cardio videos.
https://tinyurl.com/purposeforwardresources

YouTube is also a great resource for fitness videos.

Am I getting at least 7–8 hours of sleep a night? Do I have enough energy to make it through the day? Am I practicing proper sleep hygiene by only using my bedroom for sleep, avoiding electronics before bed, and going to bed and waking up at consistent times? Because without proper rest, you are certainly not your best self.

_____

_____

_____

_____

_____

Note that there are several apps that will track your sleep for you. Feel free to investigate!

You may even want to consider introducing massage to feel better in your body and balance out exercising. (Think foam rollers, chirp wheels, and a good old self-massage!). Maybe you have a massage gift certificate hanging around from your last birthday. Go put it to use, will ya?! (Or send it to me. I will gladly use it up for you! ☺)

PHYSICAL HEALTH

Do I attend my annual physicals and check-ups? (This may include your primary care doctor, dentist, eye doctor, dermatologist, women's/men's health screenings.) Am I ensuring that I am taking all the necessary medications as prescribed?

_____

_____

_____

_____

Am I being mindful of my weight, fat, and sugar intake? How about my consumption of alcohol, drugs, and tobacco? Do I need to make any adjustments?

_____

_____

_____

_____

_____

_____

FINANCES

How do I define financial stability? Do I feel good about the money I am receiving and how I am spending it? Do I have a budget? Maybe it's something you need to work on creating or modifying.

_____

_____

_____

_____

_____

_____

Beautiful!

Know that there are a multitude of resources available out there that cover these topics in much more detail. I know that you are smart and that you can Google. So it's on you to follow up and follow through on any action steps you need to implement. I believe in you!

Remember, sometimes we need to get out of our heads and into our bodies. Thinking about the next steps in life is all-consuming. It is a very heady process. To balance it out, we need to step away from all the cognition and physically get into our bodies.

I once had a client who was feeling very "blocked" in terms of having enough ambition to look for a job. After checking in with her on what her life looks like when she is NOT looking for a job, we realized that what was lacking was just her being healthy. She needed physical fitness to start feeling better and to gain more energy.

Her "homework" changed from job hunting to going to the gym 3–4 days a week with a buddy. Getting physically healthier as well as having a support system and gaining more confidence was the missing piece that she needed to launch herself forward!

That was a big aha moment for me and really emphasized the importance of approaching career coaching in a holistic way. And to be honest, it was most likely the catalyst that transitioned me from being "just" a life purpose & career coach to a *holistic* life purpose & career coach.

Ok. Take some time to look back over your responses.

What is in and out of balance?

_____

_____

Notice any gaps and where you can invite in some balance.

_____

_____

List 1–3 things you can do to make sure you are well represented in the physical domain.

This is an important one, because remember—lack of balance in the other areas will show up here as well! You MAY just be able to begin to "fix" them from here!! ☺

I may have just saved you hundreds of dollars in therapy bills! You're welcome!!

1. _____

2. _____

3. _____

Now, let's drop into your body and experience a bit of mindfulness. I'm going to lead you through a meditation for each of these sections. For your convenience, in addition to the text, I've also included links to spoken recordings of each of these exercises, so there's no excuse for not giving them a shot!

MINDFULNESS CORNER
THE FIVE SENSES

Listen here: https://tinyurl.com/purposeforwardresources

Take a moment to close your eyes and take a deep breath, inhaling through your nose and exhaling through your mouth.

Now, focus on what you can see around you. Take note of the colors and images that come into view.

Next, shift your attention to what you can hear. Listen carefully for any sounds, whether it's the rumbling of your stomach or distant noises.

Try to identify any scents that may be present in the air—maybe the smell of freshly cut grass, the smell of rain, or the cookies that were just baked.

Now notice if there are any lingering tastes in your mouth. (Those cookies, maybe?)

Now, pay attention to your sense of touch. Feel the clothes against your skin, the hair on your neck, and even any emotions that you may be experiencing.

Observe all these sensations as they arise in your body. Take about five minutes to simply sit and feel.

How do you feel now? ♥

Nice!! I hope you feel a bit more relaxed and present in your body.

Now that you are committed to going to the gym, sneaking in a bit more yoga, and getting eight hours of sleep, it's time to shimmy over to the next layer—the cognitive domain. I promise I'll try not to make it too "heady"!

COGNITIVE

My mind not only wanders. It sometimes leaves completely!

WHAT IS THE COGNITIVE DOMAIN?

YOUR BRAIN. YOUR THINKING MIND. This domain is all about how your mind works and processes information. And that's pretty important when you are looking for work.

This domain covers the stuff like

- Perception (how you see and hear things)

- Attention (what you focus on)

- Memory

- Reasoning (solving puzzles like a pro)

- Problem-solving (cracking those tricky challenges)

- Decision-making (choosing your path wisely)

- Language skills (your way with words!)

The cognitive domain includes finding harmony and peace in your thoughts. It includes our

- Self-image
- Beliefs
- Values
- Goals
- Overall mindset
- Self-expression

Practices such as meditation, practicing gratitude, and taking part in self-help and therapy when needed are pathways to improved cognitive health.

The best part? All these cognitive processes don't just stay in your brain; they interact with your body and emotions! The intricate connection between your mind and emotions is well established through scientific research. The strong relationship between cognitive processes and emotional experiences has been extensively studied and validated.

What challenges do I currently have in my life? What are they teaching me?

_____

_____

_____

_____

_____

_____

Notice your mindset. Are you an overall positive person, a realist, a pessimist, or somewhere in between? What is the purpose of your mindset? Do you like how you are showing up in this area??

Think back to chapter 2. Do I have any limiting beliefs? Does the belief serve me and my highest good? If I were to let go of the belief, who would I become? (Be honest here. It's OK.)

_____

_____

_____

_____

_____

Let's talk about technology-related boundaries for a moment. Think about how you deal with managing the overload of information we have access to. Notice what kind of boundaries (or lack thereof) that you have for yourself around technology. Feel free to refer to my blog on technology boundaries here: https://tinyurl.com/ purposeforwardresources

And believe me when I tell you, this is something many of us need to work on.

Do I take enough mental breaks throughout the day? (This includes taking breaks from technology to promote mental well-being and to reduce digital overload). Is there a way I could invite in more opportunities for my mind to be at ease? (Focusing on my heart beating, staring into space.)

_____

_____

_____

_____

_____

What is something new I would like to learn to keep my brain engaged?

_____

_____

_____

_____

_____

_____

What are the top three things I am grateful for? Having a daily gratitude practice is a real game changer in terms of shifting your cognitive mindset.

1. _____

2. _____

3. _____

It's also so helpful to think about the company you keep. Perhaps there are ways to surround yourself more with positive people and encouraging influences and distance yourself from negativity.

Nice job thinking about how you think! ☺

Now, glance back over your answers. Are there any adjustments you can make to bring more equilibrium to this area?

1. _____

2. _____

3. _____

YES!! I can't wait to hear about how you made more effort to rest your mind, and how it changed your life!

Now it's time to take a little time for yourself with some mindfulness.

MINDFULNESS CORNER
GUIDED IMAGERY

Listen here: https://tinyurl.com/ purposeforwardresources

Gently bring your eyes to a close and drop into your body.

Really let yourself drop in. Let allll of those muscles completely relax.

Now, imagine a vast, breathtakingly beautiful sky, painted in serene shades of blue.

It stretches out infinitely.

Now envision this vast sky as your mind, each thought a calm cloud.

Observe the clouds (the thoughts), as they gracefully glide through the sky that is your mind.

Witness them without judgment or attachment.

Take about five deep and nourishing breaths, inhaling serenity, and exhaling any tension or stress.

Feel your belly rise as you inhale and release as you exhale.

With each breath, allow the clouds to gently dissolve, leaving behind a sense of calm clarity.

> *Maybe eventually all that is left is blue sky.*
>
> *Embrace this moment of deep connection.*
>
> *Close your eyes and enjoy this sense of mental peace for a few moments. Just sit and be.*
>
> *How do you feel now?*♥

Great!! I hope you feel a bit more calmness in your mind and you are feeling like you are in a good place.

Time to dive into the emotional realm, Purpose Seeker!

But first—take a brain break if you need it. You've earned it!

EMOTIONAL

"There's a crack in everything. That's how the light gets in."

—Leonard Cohen

WHAT IS THE EMOTIONAL DOMAIN?

O HH, THIS CAN BE A touchy one! Do you feel the sensitivity here?!

This realm is where your emotions are the boss and call the shots on how you experience life and make decisions, especially when it comes to finding the perfect career path.

And it's a colorful medley of feelings, for sure!

It's where happiness, excitement, and passion shine, and where challenges like stress and anxiety also manifest. This domain is all about understanding how your emotions guide you, influence your choices, and impact your interactions with others.

As a career starter, exploring the emotional domain can be a game changer. It's like unlocking the secret to your own emotional superpowers! By understanding and managing your emotions, you'll gain confidence, build strong relationships, and make choices that truly resonate with your heart's desires. And ultimately get to your purpose!

The emotional domain includes recognizing, processing, and releasing emotions in a healthy way, being free from negative emotions you have experienced in the past, and having the ability to give and receive love. It includes being a part of a community, having a good relationship with yourself, and seeking emotional support in relationships when needed, including family, friends, and romantic relationships.

It is also feeling seen.

It is an important skill to learn to slow down and listen to your emotions. Your emotions are communicating with you, providing valuable insight into your interests, passions, and values. For example, you may feel sadness as a result of having lost something or someone. That sadness is communicating to you something important to you, something that matters to you; otherwise, that loss wouldn't resonate emotionally. Just like if you have an encounter that sparks joy, you should pay attention to what brought on that emotion and reflect on how to duplicate it. Because we want more of that!

OK, it's reflection time! (Are you still with me?!)

What are some experiences or encounters in my life that bring a sense of excitement, joy, happiness, or curiosity? What is this communicating to me about my passions or what areas I should pursue?

_____

_____

_____

_____

_____

_____

What are some experiences or encounters that bring on negative emotions such as sadness, pain, worry, angst? What is this communicating to me about what I should avoid or minimize my connection with? Or about what I should be pursuing instead?

_____

_____

_____

_____

_____

_____

Do I feel seen and understood by my friends, family, my significant other? Do I feel good about the people in my life? What, if any, adjustments may I need to make in this area?

_____

_____

_____

_____

_____

_____

Also, notice your relationship with yourself. Do you take care of yourself?

Do I feel connected to my community? Is there more I can do here to feel a part of something larger than myself? (No worries if you are not. We can't get a perfect score on everything.)

_____

_____

_____

_____

_____

_____

Just as we seek a physician's help when our body is sick, it's equally important to consider therapy when we could use some support with stress, depression, or anxiety. It's about taking care of your whole self.

Am I holding on to any negative emotions from the past? Could I benefit from therapy? Do I have any healing that needs to take place?

_____

_____

_____

_____

_____

_____

Notice if they are your emotions, someone else's, or the world's.

Great work! It's not always fun to dive into the emotional realm; there's usually quite a bit of "stuff" that accumulates here.

Now take a glance back at your answers. What is in and out of balance here—anything?

Lots of stuff can show up here. Don't be surprised if this domain feels the most raw and vulnerable. Totally normal!

Think of 1–3 things you can do to make sure you are well embodied in the emotional domain. What are a few remarkable things you can do to change your life?!

1. _____

2. _____

3. _____

I can't wait to see how your life is going to change now that you are going to find more down time to go to therapy to heal that emotional baggage. You are on a roll!

Now it's time for another opportunity for mindfulness. Get comfortable!

MINDFULNESS CORNER
EMOTIONAL AWARENESS

Listen here: https://tinyurl.com/ purposeforwardresources

Find a comfortable position in your seat, allowing yourself to relax. Feel the firm connection of your feet with the ground, anchoring you in this present moment. Take a moment to notice your heartbeat, your breath, and the circulation flowing through your body.

Now, turn your attention inward to your emotions. How are you feeling right now? Take a moment to observe without getting caught up in any stories or judgments. There's no need to label your emotions; just accept them as they are in this present moment.

Shift your focus to love. Hold this feeling in your awareness, taking a few breaths to embrace it fully. Allow love to surround you.

Next, bring your attention to peace. Notice what peace feels like within you, and simply be at peace for a moment.

Now, let joy fill your being. Experience joy without any hurry, just allowing yourself to be fully present in this joyful state.

Take a few moments to sit in stillness, breathing naturally, and witness any sensations, feelings, or thoughts that arise.

When you feel ready, gently bring your meditation to a close and return to your day with a sense of calm and overall centeredness.

Beautiful work! I hope you are feeling good, my friend. I am proud of you!

On to the spiritual!

SPIRITUAL

"Finding oneself, one finds the meaning of life, the significance of life, the joy of life, the splendor of life. Finding oneself is the greatest finding in man's life, and this finding is only possible when you are alone. When your consciousness is not crowded by anything, by anybody, when your consciousness is utterly empty— in that emptiness, in that nothingness, a miracle happens."

—Osho

WHAT IS THE SPIRITUAL DOMAIN?

NOW THAT YOU'VE HAD SOME time to reflect on the physical, cognitive, and emotional aspects of wellness, let's explore the spiritual domain—an incredibly unique one! Here we will further explore the power of mediation, a secret weapon to help unlock your purpose.

As a yoga teacher, I'm pretty fired up about this section, and I hope you are too! The spiritual domain involves connecting with a higher power and nurturing your soul. This can take various forms, such as engaging in spiritual or religious practices or simply immersing yourself in nature's beauty. It's an experience of connection with God, a higher power, your higher self, consciousness, collective consciousness, or even energy—a path that brings us back to wholeness. (Choose the term that resonates with you!)

There are no limits to the various ways we can connect with our spiritual selves. It may take the form of dancing like no one is watching, meditating, being creative, or simply being still.

It's about checking in with yourself on a soul level, but the real challenge is being quiet enough to listen.

Sometimes, finding that quiet time is a challenge, right? Yet, if you manage to create a little space for yourself, you might catch a gentle nudge or moment of intuition, leading you toward what you're truly meant to do. It could be creating a tune on the piano, joining a stress-relieving yoga session, speaking up for what's right, or lending a listening ear to someone in need.

Don't overthink it. Embrace it. Flow with it.

Are you ready to assess the spiritual?

Let's do it! My intention is that these prompts will plant the seeds for living more in alignment with your higher self (connecting with your innate wisdom and authenticity) and true purpose.

How do I define spirituality? How do I embrace spirituality or religion in my life (or do I?)

_____

_____

_____

_____

_____

_____

_____

How could I connect with a larger community on this aspect of who I am? Is this something I would want to integrate if I am not already doing it? What might that look like? (Know that this is totally optional!)

_____

_____

_____

_____

_____

One timeless way to connect with our spiritual side is through nature. Just in case this box didn't get checked above, I am asking here to be sure of it!

Nature is the oldest medicine. It is ingrained in our animalistic human nature, and for that reason, it never goes out of style. Take a walk, smell the smells, maybe even feel your bare feet on the earth. It sounds so simple and obvious, but I promise it is one of the most impactful things you can do.

So, tell me, how do you welcome nature into your life? Could you do more of it?

_____

_____

_____

_____

_____

_____

Those are some beautiful reflections.

Did you know that creativity can serve as a gateway to connecting with the spiritual domain?

Fun fact: Creativity is the #2 skill requested by employers! So, this is an important skill to continue to cultivate. The best part? The more we use creativity, the more it grows!

How do I define creativity, and what do I most want to create? How do I define play for myself?

_____

_____

_____

_____

_____

_____

Now, read back over your responses. What is in balance and out of balance in the spiritual domain? Notice any gaps. How can you bring in more equilibrium here?

1. _____

2. _____

3. _____

I'm excited to hear about your follow-through and how your life will evolve! Maybe you'd like to create a special time for yourself—a mini-retreat tailored to the things you really enjoy. You could do things that make you feel good, like gentle movement or a bit of meditation, to connect with a higher power. Ending it with some journaling could bring more clarity to your life. Now, it's time for a meditation.

MINDFULNESS CORNER
SPIRITUAL ENLIGHTENMENT

Listen here: https://tinyurl. com/purposeforwardresources

Close your eyes and bring your attention to your breath.

Feel your belly rise on the inhale and fall on the exhale.

Go ahead; really let that belly expand and release.

Take a deep breath in for 4 counts, hold it for 4 counts, then exhale for 4 counts.

Keep your attention on this belly breathing for a few breaths.

Now, connect with your higher self. Invite them in and trust their guidance. Know that you are in a safe place.

Place your hand on your heart and feel a profound sense of purpose within.

Ask yourself, "Who am I really?" and listen for the answer.

Then, inquire about your purpose in life.

Sit quietly for a few moments without distractions and notice what comes up. It might be a word, a phrase, an image, or a feeling.

Embrace this moment of deep connection with your inner self. Enjoy the sense of spiritual integration for a few moments. Just sit and be.

Now, how do you feel? ❤

Beautiful job! You are well on your journey to unlocking your true purpose. I hope you feel a bit more clarity within your spirit and carry it into the rest of your day!

Another note on self-care: From my own experience leading yoga and wellness retreats, taking the time to explore self-care across the four domains (physical, cognitive, emotional, and spiritual) often helps people see things more clearly. And remember, it doesn't have to be a big, formal undertaking. Just find 60–90 minutes in your schedule every now and then, maybe once every couple of months, to reconnect with yourself and the amazing physical, cognitive, emotional, and spiritual person you are inside.

Because all the answers lie in you.

And you know what? It's true that trying to embrace all these domains daily or weekly can be a challenge. But if you ever feel a bit out of sync, take a moment to examine if there's an area you've been neglecting or have yet to explore. That missing piece might be the key to getting your groove back. And hey, don't forget about yoga—it might just be the shortcut to all of this! (Of course, I might be a bit biased.)

A NOTE ABOUT YOGA

I want you to know something about yoga.

(Brace yourself as I step onto my soapbox for a moment!)

Yoga is for EVERYONE. It doesn't matter what your body shape, fitness level, gender, age, ethnicity, or social status is. Can't touch your toes? No problem; you're normal. Struggle with balance? You're not alone. Racing mind? Welcome to the club.

In yoga practice, we show up to be present in our bodies, connect with our breath, and release a little stress. Sure, it enhances strength, flexibility, and balance, but the true transformation lies in mindfulness. The real effort is showing up, pushing ourselves within our OWN healthy limits, and listening to what OUR bodies need, even if it means a gentle, supported child's pose.

Let me tell you this: Waiting to be thinner, stronger, or more flexible to join a yoga class means missing out on the wisdom, stillness, and mental strength it offers.

Of course, repeated practice of various stretching and balancing exercises can elicit positive changes in your body, but that's not what real yoga is about. Real yoga is about showing up for yourself, taking what you need from your mat, and carrying it into your life. It's about self-discovery, growth, and finding balance on and off the mat.

HOW TO GET A YOGA BODY

1. Have a Body

2. Do Yoga

Even the self-discovery process that is this book is a great example. That's yoga, baby!

So don't wait—start your yoga journey today, exactly as you are.

It can be quite helpful to engage in yoga prior to meditation, as it prepares the body to relax and sit comfortably. The physical postures and breathing exercises release tension and help you feel more at ease. By practicing yoga beforehand, you create a peaceful and focused state of mind, making meditation easier and more enjoyable.

Now let me introduce you to something called samadhi, which we can (potentially) find through practicing meditation.

SAMADHI: WHAT IT IS AND WHY IT IS HELPFUL TO FINDING YOUR PURPOSE

During meditation, it's possible to experience an incredibly tranquil and reenergizing state called samadhi. I fondly remember a time before having children when I would get out of bed in the morning, ease into the day, and immediately begin meditating. Mornings are ideal for meditation, as the mind is clear and distractions are few. During these sessions, I was able to achieve a deep state of meditation that could be identified as samadhi. Surprisingly, I also experienced it once during "flotation therapy," floating weightlessly in saltwater. It may sound a bit hokey, but I assure you, it's real!

Samadhi is a state of profound meditation where you experience a deep sense of oneness, inner peace, and connection with the universal consciousness. It is a state of complete absorption, where the mind becomes still, and you transcend the boundaries of the ego, merging with the object of meditation. It is essentially the culmination of the meditation process.

Let me lead you through a meditation practice here, one that will help you connect with your higher self, and ultimately your purpose.

I absolutely can't move on from this section without sharing something I once heard from a Laughter Yoga instructor (yes, it's a real thing!).

At the intersection of physical, cognitive, emotional, and spiritual domains lie the 5 Elements of Joy—powerful practices that enrich our well-being and foster a sense of happiness and fulfillment. Embracing these elements can have profound effects on our overall health, nurturing every aspect of our being.

THE 5 ELEMENTS OF JOY CHALLENGE

The 5 Elements of Joy are the key ingredients to ensuring we experience joy in our lives. They include singing, laughing, dancing, playing, and gratitude.

You don't have to do them all at once (although that would be pretty awesome!). I once challenged myself to experience one of these elements each day for five days (and post about it on social). By the end of the challenge, I felt noticeably more joyful. I dare you to take on this challenge too! Embrace the power of singing, laughing, dancing, playing, and expressing gratitude daily, and watch how it brightens your days with joy and positivity. Give it a try and see the magic unfold in your life!

Hopefully you now have a clearer pathway to access wholeness in your own life, through finding the "conversation" between your physical, cognitive, emotional, and spiritual realms. It may be helpful to look back and see which domains may need a bit more love and which ones you are already giving proper attention to.

As we've discussed, laying the groundwork to access your purpose is vital. Taking the time to reflect on different aspects of your life holistically is crucial. Setting intentions is equally important.

WHAT'S NEXT

So, let's pause here and set an intention for the next part of this book: finding your purpose. Really immerse yourself in it. What do you want to achieve? How will life transform once you declare your purpose?

The majority of the work lies in imagining the outcome.

Now that you have a solid foundation of self-care and feel good physically, mentally, emotionally, and spiritually, it's time for what you came for—finding your purpose. Get ready to dig in and explore the transformational journey of discovering (and declaring) your purpose.

So go ahead and take a deep breath in. Tense all of the muscles in your body for about 20 seconds. Now shake it out, relax those muscles, and release that tension with a big, generous exhale!

Take a moment to pause as you get ready to enter the chapter that has lots of love wrapped around it. (I know because I infused my heart into it as I wrote it.)

CHAPTER 5

MY LIFE STORY

"There is a vitality, a life force, an energy, a quickening that is translated through you into action, and because there is only one of you in all of time, this expression is unique. And if you block it, it will never exist through any other medium and it will be lost. The world will not have it. It is not your business to determine how good it is nor how valuable nor how it compares with other expressions. It is your business to keep it yours clearly and directly, to keep the channel open."

—Martha Graham

T HIS QUOTE JUST SPEAKS TO my soul. Does it for you too?

Take a look at this book cover for a moment. (It is gorgeous, isn't it?! ☺). Notice that radiant light illuminating the crown of her head? That's the crown chakra—where divine wisdom and universal energy unite. The light source connects directly with it. This image serves as a wonderful metaphor for grasping the concept of purpose and how it connects with our life story.

Our calling is the spark that ignites us and launches us into action.

I have discovered that a powerful method to clarify our purpose is the process of creating a written narrative of our unique and personal life story. Understanding our story and recognizing the meaningful synchronicities we've encountered helps to fortify our understanding of who we are and who we need to be. That is what we are going to dive into in this chapter.

You are inching closer to putting words to your unique dharma. We are purpose-activated the moment we grasp our purpose and consciously live it, being attuned to HOW we present ourselves to the world and the deliberate actions we take. But first—it's time to uncover your life synchronicities!

SYNCHRONICITIES

"Synchronicity is an ever present reality for those who have eyes to see."

—Carl Jung

YOU STILL WITH ME, PURPOSE Seeker? I need you to do one thing for me. I need you to keep your mind wide open and just humor me for the first part of this section because we are going to get into something that some may consider a little out there. But trust me, it's tried, tested, and effective. And we're going for it!

I'm talking about synchronicities.

WHAT ARE SYNCHRONICITIES?

These are chance events, otherwise known as coincidences. Meaningful coincidences that seem to occur in a way that suggests a deeper connection between events, even if there is no apparent causal relationship.

It is human nature to attach meaning to events. Ever heard of something called confirmation bias?

It's the cognitive tendency to notice and remember information that confirms your existing beliefs or expectations. In other words, it acts as an internal mechanism that encourages you to trust your own intuition!

We are also wired to recognize patterns, even in unrelated events, as well as to have selective perception (seeing what we want to see to affirm what we ultimately want).

Maybe it's the time your friend told you about a new book and you accidentally knocked it off the bookshelf at the store. Or the former coworker that popped in your head and suddenly reached out and invited you to Paint and Vino out of the blue.

I once had a client who made the bold and brave decision to move across the country in pursuit of finding a location for her career to flourish. As fate would have it, when she began house-hunting in her new location, she stumbled upon a pretty amazing coincidence: The house number of one of the homes she viewed was IDENTICAL to the one she had left behind. What an extraordinary reminder that she was indeed on the right path! (And, just so you know, she decided to make that house her new home!)

Here are some examples from my own life that I can share as examples:

1. I really wanted to learn how to swing dance, and I kept telling everyone about it. Then, the very next week, a new employee was hired at my company. Guess what? He was actually a swing dance teacher! It felt like a fortunate coincidence. One that was meant for me. He showed me the ropes by introducing me to the swing scene, including where to take lessons and where I could be a part of the social dances. The rest is history, and I became a swing dancer (and even performed!). Swing dancing became an integral part of who I was and served a purpose beyond just having fun. It helped

me relax my mind, learn to follow someone else's lead, and let me express myself creatively.

2. My husband and I bought a home a while back. Interestingly, the seller was a lovely woman who had a career in higher education career development—exactly the field I was striving to get into. What's even more remarkable is that she extended an invitation for an informational interview right at her workplace, offering a notable gesture of support and connection.

   And that's just the beginning. During one of my yoga classes, I experienced a delightful twist of fate. The yoga teacher noticed my address on my intake form and shared that she used to live in the exact same house!

   Considering my strong interest in both higher education and yoga, this felt like a powerful indication that this house (and these careers) were meant for me.

3. I've always professed that quality time is my love language. Isn't it fascinating that I met my husband just a few hours after he conquered the most arduous (and last) exam of his life to attain the title of licensed psychologist? He had dedicated years to his education and preparation for that very moment. It's a testament that he was not only the one for me, but that destiny timed our meeting impeccably, for meeting him without the prospect of quality time wouldn't have been suitable for someone who values it as much as I do!

   Interestingly, my husband is an integral part of my professional journey too, as he is so very supportive of my endeavors (I can be an ambitious one!). I mention this because I firmly believe that fate led me not only to a soul mate in love but also to a partner who encourages me to pursue my dreams and continually evolve to be the best human I can be. Which is something that I believe to be very important to my personal and professional growth. The alignment of these elements continues to leave me in awe. In fact, it's as if the universe held up a radiant sign that read, "This is your person!!"

Now that I've shared a bit about me to get you warmed up...

Your turn.

If you think about it, I'm sure you can relate. There are synchronicities in your own life. And they might just have something important to tell you.

Here are some meaningful coincidences I've had in my life: (If you get stuck, remember your "setting the foundation" tools. Maybe you need to get out of your head and into your body. Go for a walk or dance around a bit first. ☺)

1. _____

2. _____

3. _____

4. _____

Now, what are some things that these synchronicities are confirming for me, or leading me towards? (Think in terms of affirming passions, relationships, or career paths.)

_____

_____

_____

_____

_____

_____

_____

_____

_____

_____

_____

_____

_____

_____

_____

_____

_____

_____

_____

_____

_____

_____

_____

Now we are going to pivot into thinking about the narrative that your life is telling.

LIFE STORY EXAMPLES

*"The two most important days in your life are the day
you are born, and the day you find out why."*

—Mark Twain

A S YOU START TO THINK about what your personal
life story entails, it's helpful to draw inspiration from
the accounts of others. Let's look at some examples
written by some of my real-life clients who were so gracious to
vulnerably share their own life stories.

Let's start with Caite.

CAITE'S LIFE STORY:

*"All my life, I've had a Type-A personality—striving
for perfection, doubting myself, and struggling with
anxiety. I can recall time and time again seeking out
ways to keep my anxiety at bay, from seeing a therapist
in college to implementing a regimented meditation
routine, and even reading the Bible. All of these strategies helped me cope for the time being.*

*Then, with having a baby, one of the biggest changes
a person goes through in their lives, coupled with the
raging hormones, my anxiety came back with a ven-
geance. What I have learned through the joy, tears,*

and trials of being a mother, however, is that I have a different purpose in life now. My purpose is not to necessarily make sure that my child (and perhaps future children) are always happy, but rather, for them to know that they are loved unconditionally. While this may seem like a daunting task, when I see my life from this perspective, it makes my anxiety seem so small.

While anxiety may be something that I always struggle with, knowing that I have a bigger purpose in my life reminds me that I am not my anxiety. It cannot control me anymore."

The Title of Caite's Life as a Book or Movie:

I Am Enough

Now, let's meet Sandra.

SANDRA'S LIFE STORY:

"I am a Latina woman who broke through generational chains because I know that I am worthy of a good and enriched life. I defied all odds by taking every season of my life and using them as lessons, rather than setbacks. Because of this, I have discovered self-awareness, gratitude, generosity, and inspiration through my lessons. I juggle many hats, each of which I am proud of: a mother, a manager, an entrepreneur, and a volunteer. My motto is 'Giving back is one of the greatest gifts that anyone can possess. It provides endless abundance in every aspect of human life.'"

The Title of Sandra's Life as a Book or Movie:

The Season of Life: In Pursuit of Abundance

I want to thank both of these beautiful souls for giving me permission to share their sacred and very personal words. Your incredible journeys inspire others to follow their dreams as well!

Now it's your turn.

WRITING MY LIFE STORY

*"I trust the next chapter of my life because I am
the author who will write its ending."*

—Narin Grewall

I F YOU WERE TO TAKE a few moments to think about the major life-changing events of your life, notice what comes to mind. These may be milestones, thresholds, or events that changed the way you look at life. It can include any major challenges or successes and can even include things like relationships and personal growth.

Some examples may be graduating a program, making a team, losing a job, entering or exiting a relationship, experiencing grief, physical ailments, parenthood, relocating, etc.

Starting at birth, write a list (or draw a map or timeline) of all the significant events that have happened until now. (If you are not sure if you should include it, go ahead and put it down. You can always adjust it later.) It may end up being 3–5 major events that stand out in your mind.

MY PERSONAL TIMELINE OF SIGNIFICANT EVENTS:

_____

_____

Melissa M. Carvalho, M.A., RYT

Whew! How about that trip down memory lane?!

Now, with these major life events fresh in your mind, can you form a narrative that tells the story of your life to this point? Compose a synopsis that summarizes your personal journey, similar to the examples above. Notice any patterns or themes in your life events. What life lessons have you learned along the way? What specific challenges have you overcome? What story is your life telling?

You are the author of your own life story.

I encourage you to really take your time with this one. Maybe reflect on it during a walk or a meditation. You may even want to grab a journal so you can take up as much space as you need.

_____

_____

_____

_____

_____

_____

_____

_____

_____

_____

_____

_____

Melissa M. Carvalho, M.A., RYT

What an adventure life is, huh?!

Now take a moment to reflect on your story in THIS very moment. Who are you today in this moment and season of life?

Reflect on your challenges and your triumphs.

If someone were to ask how you are doing at this moment, and you were to give them a truthful answer, how would you describe it?

If there was just one word to sum up this time in your life, what would it be?

(I know I ask a ton of questions. Sorry, not sorry!)

Now look back at your life story and your "word" to sum up this time in your life. HOW are you telling it?

Notice the tone. Is it positive or negative? Are you a villain or a victim? Are you empowered or disempowered?

Notice if you are happy with the story you are telling.

Is there a more optimistic way to look at your situation?

The answer is a big fat YES; there always is! ☺

Consider reframing your experiences, emphasizing the lessons learned and the personal growth achieved. Reflect on the challenges as stepping stones to greater resilience and wisdom. Challenge yourself to paint a brighter picture, one where you are the hero of your story, overcoming obstacles and taking advantage of opportunities like the superhero you are.

For example, I've had the privilege of working with clients who, regrettably, have come from challenging family circumstances encompassing abuse, poverty, addiction, illness, and much more. In place of embracing the role of a victim and replaying their 'woe is me' life narrative (which, considering what they've faced, is certainly understandable), they're actively learning to retell their stories with empowerment at the forefront.

These individuals are embracing their warrior spirit, harnessing their resilience and inner strength to rise above the hands they were dealt. They're embracing their newfound values, transforming their perspective on life, and sharing the unique gifts they have to offer others. By doing this, they not only rewrite their own life narratives but also inspire others to do the same, demonstrating the power of resilience and determination.

I also want to mention something here. Maybe you are one of those folks who carries within them an absolutely heartbreaking story (many of us do). You may always carry some of that pain with you, and that's absolutely alright. But I challenge you to see if you can identify some alternative language to convey it.

Identifying alternate language to convey your experiences can help you break free from victimhood, allowing you to rewrite your narrative with greater empowerment.

Seek out the silver linings and the lessons it has given you. Your mindset, without a doubt, is one of the most potent tools you have. It's a choice. Everyday. Remember that.

There's a yoga studio I frequent that has a sign hanging in the bathroom that reads, "I think I will just choose to be happy today." This sentiment deeply resonates with me, particularly during difficult times. Sometimes, that choice is all we're left with. It's a decision we confront daily. And a little bit every day adds up to a lot.

OK, I will step off my podium now.

Look back at your story. See if it is the one you want to be telling. Are there any limiting beliefs present or anything you want to change about it?

Think about how you want to rewrite it, but this time, notice what this story is foreshadowing. How does this book or movie end? What is everything in your life leading up to?

Here is the new story I want to tell:

_____

_____

_____

_____

_____

_____

If your life were to be a book or a movie, what would the name of it be called? (Feel free to include a tagline!)

_____

_____

_____

_____

_____

_____

Now go ahead and share it with the world (trembling introverts, don't worry—this part is not mandatory!).

You have just rewritten your life story. How powerful is that?

Again, you are the author of our own life story. If the current chapter or the entire story of your life doesn't resonate with you, always remember that you have the power to rewrite it, or at least change the ending. It starts by getting clear on your intention, followed by creating actionable steps. Remember, this is a trip that is uniquely your own—there's no need to rush. It won't happen overnight. But slowly chipping away at it will get you to where you want to be: living a life with more meaning and fulfillment.

Take a few moments to digest this section. It can be a heavy one or a fun one, depending on what came up for you. All the feelings are welcome. All your emotions are welcome in this space.

This next section is "my baby," if you will. I hold it in high regard as the most dynamic part of this entire book. My aspiration for you is that you approach it from the best possible frame of mind.

So set yourself up for success. Take a self-care break if you need it. Come back when you are in a good mental place and ready to craft your life purpose statement.

This simple exercise revolutionized the way I interact with life. It made me accountable for the dharma I carry and the commitment I have to the community around me. It was a pivotal moment in my life when I "woke up" and found the ability to authentically express, wholeheartedly embrace, and ultimately "activate" my purpose.

And now, the spotlight is on you. (Have I told you how delighted I am that you are taking this journey for yourself?!)

Big hugs.

STEP 3

FINDING MY PURPOSE

CHAPTER 6

LIFE GUIDANCE STATEMENTS

*"Life is like looking for your phone. Most
of the time it's in your hand."*

—Unknown

NOW THAT THE DRINKS, APPS, and salad have been served, it's time for the main course! (I need to stop writing while I am hungry, I know!)

Putting your purpose into words helps you to clarify the legacy you want to leave behind (we can't live forever, right?!).

It helps to guide your actions and decisions toward the goal of fostering a positive impact on the world. It also enhances your ability to articulate your mission effectively, gives you a clear sense of direction, and significantly amplifies your motivation to live it out fully.

Now, let's write some statements that put the "what" in your life purpose!

LIFE PURPOSE: AN INTRODUCTION

"As your desire is, so is your will.
As your will is, so is your deed.
As your deed is, so is your destiny."

—*Brihadaranyaka Upanishad (IV.4.5)*

HERE IS AN INTRIGUING THING about purpose: There can be a whole boatload of us out there that do the same thing for work. Take, for instance, the role of a science teacher. It's conceivable that you might cover identical subjects and stick to the same curriculum as countless others. But the WAY you teach it is going to be very unique to you and give a very different experience to your students. That is what our unique purpose does for us. It takes on its own signature aroma, and no two will ever be the same.

If you don't choose to honor your truest essence and do the sacred work you were born to do, no one else will do it. It won't ever exist in that way anywhere else for anyone else.

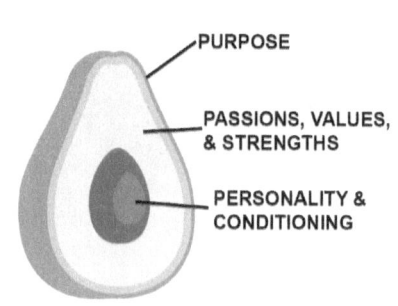

Do you remember the pic of the avocado in chapter 3? Let's revisit it, shall we?

Purpose is that part of us that is displayed to the world. Knowing our identity, being aware of our passions, values, and strengths—all of this holds tremendous significance. But its true value comes when we convert this insight into action, effectively communicating and offering our dharma to the world.

WHAT ARE SOME EXAMPLES OF LIFE PURPOSE?

We all define the meaning of life in different ways. For some, it's about having fun; for some, it's about relationships; for some, it's about being the best version of ourselves. Understanding our purpose and the way we tell our life story helps us live our life ON purpose. It's what gets you out of bed in the morning and keeps you going. It is knowing, with certainty, that the way you expend your life force energy is in alignment with your highest calling and contribution to the world.

What does purpose look like? It can take the shape of many things:

• Providing for your family

• Exploring different cultures

• Championing environmental preservation

• Creating a positive imprint on others' lives

• Cultivating a sense of satisfaction in your life

• Weaving melodies through music

• Sharing knowledge and enlightening minds

• Nurturing your family's well-being

- Teaching others to be healthy

- Expressing your creativity

- Infusing life with laughter

And the possibilities are endless! ☺

Now let's look at how we can put powerful words to our purpose so we can share it with others.

I would like to introduce you to THE single exercise that catapulted me into deeply understanding, genuinely owning, and truly "living" in alignment with my life purpose. This tool has taught me to filter out distractions and stay focused on what matters most to me. It has also elevated my self-awareness and enthusiasm for my dharma to another level.

I am very grateful to have had this transformational experience in my own life, and the intention of this book is to help you discover yours. And not just FIND it but ACTIVATE it.

What I'm referring to is the formulation of what I call a life purpose statement or a dharma statement (I tend to use the terms interchangeably). It involves creating and literally writing out a meta-statement that encapsulates who you are and what you are meant to do. It is a summary statement that serves as a guiding cornerstone for all you do in life.

You may recall from the introduction my story of being introduced to the concept of a dharma statement by my therapist/life coach. What I received from her laid the groundwork for my own personal journey in articulating my unique purpose. Before moving on to offer my own take on crafting a life purpose statement, I'd like to honor the source by sharing the precise tools that were presented to me, tools that were created and published by my brilliant therapist/coach Coral Brown (Thanks, Coral! ☺). Check them out in the box below!

The concept of dharma, often referred to as the "eternal spiritual path," has its origins in Hinduism and dates back nearly 4,000 years in India. If you'd like to delve deeper into the exploration of living in harmony with your dharma, you can find an insightful article by Coral.

Once you've established a foundational understanding of dharma, consider taking part in a mind-mapping meditation technique. Find the mentioned resources from *Yoga Journal* here: https://tinyurl.com/purposeforwardresources

The exercise presented here uses a mind-mapping meditation technique that will help you identify and align with your unique dharma and write a dharma statement!

I have developed my own unique approach to writing a life purpose statement since discovering these resources, and you, too, may eventually uncover a method that is authentic to you. That is the beauty in writing these highly personalized statements. There is no one "right" way to do it. It is as individual as each one of us.

I'm profoundly grateful to have unearthed this powerful life tool, as nothing lights me up more than witnessing the spark of clarity in a client's eyes when they eagerly share their life purpose statement with me and others in their lives. There's a certain magic that unfolds when we translate our purpose into words, as if we're declaring to the universe, "This is why we are here."

Your purpose is who you are and why you're here. It's important to know that WHO YOU ARE is different from WHAT YOU DO.

For example, you might work as a physical education instructor, but that role doesn't capture your entire identity. Your identity includes the things you discovered in the first part of this book, like your personality, upbringing, self-esteem, and your "compass," which is made up of your interests, values, and strengths.

Always remember: You are not your job, and your job is not you.

Embracing this perspective can liberate you from defining your entire identity through your career instead of learning to recognize the whole of all that you are. Your true self goes far beyond what you do for a living. While there may (and should!) be a connection between your identity and your career, it's crucial not to mistakenly believe that your entire identity or self-worth is solely defined by your job or profession.

So, while your profession might be Captain Bookkeeper by day, don't forget you can also be a Cat Cuddler Extraordinaire or a Midnight Ice Cream Champion by night! ☺

THE FOUNDATIONS OF "DHARMA," OFTEN REFERRED TO AS "LIFE PURPOSE"

In the *Rigveda* text, a cornerstone of the Vedic tradition, the concept of dharma is discussed. "Dharma" comes from the Sanskrit language and conveys the idea of a sacred vocation or sacred duty. It translates as "to hold together."

In this text, there's a powerful metaphor that unfolds—a depiction of the god Indra casting a vast net across the cosmos. At each intersection of this intricate web, a gem represents an individual soul tasked with maintaining the net's integrity.

This story beautifully illustrates the responsibility we have to capitalize on our unique gifts and talents, to uphold our part of the net. If we don't, the whole net could unravel. It's a captivating idea that our responsibility to fulfill our purpose not only benefits us but also has the potential to positively impact the entire world.

Now it's time for you to begin to reflect more deeply on your unique purpose. To help get those gears turning, I'm going to share descriptions of several broad-purpose domains that individuals commonly fit into. Keep in mind that these are SOME common categories that many people identify with. However, you might also belong to a category not mentioned here. That's absolutely fine—feel free to create your own!

The inspiration for these categories came to me while reading the book *Think Like a Monk*. In the book, author Jay Shetty referred to the Bhagavad Gita and talked about four different life purpose categories, referred to as varnas.

I took the liberty of expanding on them a bit, providing examples, and giving them names that I thought were more natural and intuitive to understand.

This is a great opportunity to get warmed up as you prepare to write your purpose statement. Take a look at the four categories below and see if one or two of them resonate with you the most.

LIFE PURPOSE DOMAINS
Educator Domain

Purpose: Bring the best out of people and their lives.

Skills: Learning, studying, sharing knowledge and wisdom.

Sample roles: Teachers, guides, coaches, mentors.

Example 1: Raising your children and nurturing your family by guiding and supporting your children's growth, imparting values, and shaping their futures.

Example 2: Teaching by guiding and inspiring students, empowering them to grow, learn, and achieve their goals.

Social Justice Domain

Purpose: Protect those who are less privileged.

Sample roles: Military, law enforcement, politics, activism.

Skills: Governing, inspiring, and engaging others. Leading people, movements, and groups.

Example 1: Preserving and protecting the environment, whether through sustainable practices, conservation efforts, or raising awareness about ecological issues.

Example 2: Fighting for social justice, equality, and human rights; advocating for marginalized communities; and working towards a fairer society.

Innovator Domain

Purpose: Provide action and movement for innovative ideas.

Sample roles: CEOs, marketing, sales, producers, entrepreneurs.

Skills: Brainstorming, networking, innovating.

Example 1: Leading your organization in developing innovative marketing solutions that help others to combat climate change and utilize clean energy alternatives for individuals around the world

Example 2: Creating pioneering solutions by building businesses that address societal needs and challenges.

Healer Domain

Purpose: Explore and experiment with new ideas to care for others.

Sample roles: Social workers, therapists, doctors, nurses, artists, caregivers.

Skills: Inventing, supporting, implementing.

Example 1: Creating art that evokes emotions, challenges societal norms, or communicates powerful messages.

Example 2: Helping others to heal and improve their well-being; making a positive impact on individual lives and society.

"Make My Own" Domain

Name:

_____

Purpose:

_____

_____

_____

Sample roles:

_____

_____

_____

Skills:

_____

_____

_____

Example:

_____

_____

_____

Which one or two life purpose domains (and sample roles) do you resonate with the most, and why? Feel free to use your creativity and add other roles (or even domains) that may not be listed.

_____

_____

_____

_____

_____

Nice work!

Can I let you in on a secret?

I've discovered that we can elevate our purpose even further by blending our passions together. When we combine our interests, our life purpose becomes even more powerful.

Take me, for instance. I blend my passions/roles of yoga, career coaching, and creating community together by offering retreats on personal transformation. It's a unique experience I offer others that capitalizes on my unique skillset and pursuits.

Now, I'm excited to see what you come up with for YOURS.

Here are some additional examples:

BLENDING TWO DHARMAS TOGETHER—EXAMPLES

Healthcare and Ecology: A nurse with environmentally friendly healthcare practices, combining medical expertise with a commitment to reducing the healthcare industry's ecological footprint.

Teaching and History: A teacher who educates students about historical and current social injustices, empowering them to become advocates for change and active participants in making social change.

Activism and Entrepreneurship: An entrepreneur who starts a business focused on producing ethically sourced and sustainable products while also using a portion of profits to support social justice initiatives.

Now, it's your turn! Can you think of ways to combine two or more of your purposes or passions?

_____

_____

_____

_____

Stumped? No worries! Even just having one purpose is pretty incredible.

Rest assured; the seeds have been sown. Whether it's tomorrow, months, or even years down the road, if you ever decide to blend them together, remember that you have the power to do just that!

Now let me share some sample dharma statements from real-life clients to get you inspired!

LIFE PURPOSE STATEMENTS FROM REAL-LIFE CLIENTS

"I live in the knowledge that every person has worth and every day has potential for growth and fun. I intend to use my life to build safe spaces for others, where they can meet with positivity and have fun. I believe I am to continue to bring people together, and to help forge a deeper interconnectivity between myself and others."

—Melissa

"I live with mindfulness and with acceptance of myself and others. I embrace uncertainty and change without judgment.

I trust and honor my intuition by releasing resistance and fear to the unknown.

I serve as an example to empower others with gratitude and compassion."

—Bridget

"My purpose is to improve the lives of others by helping them achieve their goals and aspirations, easing

their adversities, and uplifting their spirits. I will use my skills and abilities to develop collective positivity in this way through both individual and communal support. I will help pave the way for others to achieve and build upon my own achievements to better meet my purpose."

—Chuck

"I am a creative and lighthearted individual who lives with love and laughter.

I am dedicated to enriching and empowering those around me through my empathy, patience, and understanding.

I value family and connection. I am here to make the world a better place by showing others how to live gracefully."

—Alisha

A special thank you to the clients who gave me permission to showcase their very personal dharma statements.

I hope seeing examples of others' dharma statements will assist you in recognizing their unique and personalized nature.

Now, it's time to begin crafting YOURS! ☺

WRITING MY LIFE PURPOSE STATEMENT (& MOTTO)

"Ask what makes you come alive, and go do it. Because what the world needs is people who have come alive."

—Howard Thurman

NOW THAT YOU'VE HAD A chance to understand a bit about dharma and dharma statements, it's time to get ready to write your very own!

(Are you still with me?!)

You will want to be fully present for this one!

In this section, I will offer you a meditation to set the tone, as well as a "warm-up" and some reflection questions that will lead you up to writing your own life purpose statement.

We will also discuss how you can use this statement and translate it to a partner statement, a parenting statement, and (eventually, in chapter 8) derive a personal mission statement from it.

Let's begin with a meditation.

MINDFULNESS CORNER DISCOVERING YOUR LIFE PURPOSE

Listen here: https://tinyurl.com/purposeforwardresources

Begin by finding a comfortable and quiet space where you are free from distractions. Sit or lie down in a relaxed position. Close your eyes and slowly take a deep breath in, filling your lungs completely. Now exhale fully, releasing any tension or stress.

As you continue to breathe deeply, imagine yourself in a serene garden, completely surrounded by nature and all of her beauty. See the vivid colors of flowers, hear the gentle rustling of leaves, and feel the warm embrace of sunlight on your skin.

Now, allow yourself to draw your attention inward, deep within your own being, to explore your life purpose.

Here, imagine a radiant light illuminating from your heart. This light represents your inner essence, your true self.

Really sense the peace and tranquility that resides in this very moment.

As you focus on your inner light, ask yourself, "What brings me joy? What passions bring me deep satisfaction?" Let your mind wander through different significant events in your life, from your earliest memories to your present moment.

Visualize your passions, values, skills, and life story as vibrant threads weaving together to form a beautiful and unique pattern. Observe how they interconnect, creating a tapestry of your life experiences.

Now, imagine yourself on a path, and this path is your life's journey. Each step you've taken has led you to this moment. Feel the weight of your past experiences, the lessons learned, and the wisdom gained.

As you walk along this path, you approach a clearing where a serene pond reflects the sky above. The water is still and clear, mirroring the essence of your true self.

Gaze into the pond and ask, "What is my life purpose? What am I here to do?" Allow the ripples of your questions to settle. Notice how your heart responds.

Listen closely to your inner voice. It may come as a whisper or a clear statement. Trust your intuition. Your purpose is uniquely yours, and it's here within you, waiting to be acknowledged.

As you contemplate your purpose, remember that it may evolve and change throughout your life's journey. Embrace this growth with an open heart, knowing that each step you take aligns you more closely with your true path.

Now, take a deep breath and gently return your awareness to the present moment. When you are ready, open your eyes.

Beautiful! My intention is that this exercise may have given you a bit more insight into your purpose. Because remember, **purpose cannot be found through intellect alone.**

We often need exercises that involve the more creative and intuitive side of our brain. Especially when we are doing something as big-picture as crafting some powerful life-clarifying statements.

Without further ado …

LIFE PURPOSE MOTTO

Before you write out your life purpose statement, we are going to start with an exercise that will help you to unleash your life purpose "motto," if you will. Think of this as a simple phrase that is a warm-up to the more elaborative statement.

Now let's get to it.

Here is the simple formula:

LIFE PURPOSE MOTTO FORMULA:
(ACTION VERB) (VALUE)

Here are some examples of what it may look like: Impact Wellness, Elevate Service, Enrich Nature, Activate Purpose, Enrich Financial Wellness, Build Family, Create Art.

Use some inspiration from the charts below (or make up your own to fit!)

This list is intentionally presented in a random order, not to persuade you in any particular direction but to encourage exploration and creativity in your choices.

ACTION VERBS

Drive	Flourish	Fortify	Navigate
Transform	Educate	Cultivate	Contribute
Nurture	Embrace	Radiate	Revitalize
Renew	Demonstrate	Share	Generate

Create	Innovate	Inspire	Empower
Lead	Impact	Serve	Foster
Guide	Motivate	Advocate	Initiate
Engage	Collaborate	Build	Mobilize
Connect	Encourage	Elevate	Amplify
Develop	Challenge	Enrich	Ignite
Facilitate	Shape	Sustain	Promote
Strengthen	Pioneer	Evoke	Dedicate
Impart	Unite	Lead	Influence
Restore	Empathize	Pursue	Overcome
Organize	Spearhead	Expand	Dream
Champion	Envision	Transform	Illuminate
Support	Shape	Celebrate	Progress
Implement	Dedicate	Transcend	Aspire
Impact	Synergize	Propel	Engage
Foster	Mobilize	Bridge	Catalyze

Let's revisit our Values Table:

Peace	Positivity	Creativity	Humility
Mastery	Joy	Nature	Choice
Support	Mastery	Integrity	Tolerance
Clarity	Innovation	Spontaneity	Love
Wisdom	Gratitude	Autonomy	Compassion
Equality	Self-Respect	Curiosity	Serenity
Adventure	Pride	Wellness	Devotion
Security	Honesty	Respect	Responsibility
Relaxation	Service	Learning	Play
Truth	Patience	Harmony	Persistence
Friendship	Authenticity	Power	Competency

Melissa M. Carvalho, M.A., RYT

Ambition	Action	Grace	Personal Growth
Pleasure	Trust	Humor	Passion
Achievement	Health	Calmness	Loyalty
Diversity	Community	Education	Faith
Stability	Strength	Truth	Optimism
Family	Enthusiasm	Productivity	Kindness
Abundance	Beauty	Generosity	Balance
Cooperation	Contentment	Leadership	Openness
Empathy	Intelligence	Spirituality	Discipline

My life purpose motto is (Action verb + Motto):

_____

_____

_____

_____

Very cool!

Now it's time to jump into some reflection questions to prepare us for our life purpose statement.

REFLECTION QUESTIONS TO CREATE YOUR LIFE PURPOSE STATEMENT

Some of these questions you addressed earlier in the book, but since they are so important, let's revisit them to give them the attention they deserve.

This is what gets me going in the morning. This is what gets me excited to get out of my cozy, warm bed and face the world. (To give you some examples, maybe it's learning something new, caring for someone else, achieving something, exercising, or spending time in nature.):

_____

_____

_____

_____

_____

_____

What keeps me up at night? (This is what you spend a lot of time thinking about. Maybe it's relationships, purpose, financial security, your health, personal growth, regrets, creative ideas, the meaning of life, or world issues). The things that concern you highlight what's important to you. For example, if you spend a lot of time thinking about relationships, that means relationships are significant to you.

_____

_____

_____

_____

_____

_____

_____

I'm going to let you in on another secret...

Oftentimes, it is your wounds that can help reveal your purpose. These points of pain hold a unique kind of magic that we can share with others.

Now take a moment to reflect on your life story. What were the pain points that came up?

My wounds include:

_____

_____

_____

_____

_____

_____

_____

Here are some ways I can transform my pain into teaching, healing, or inspiring others:

_____

_____

_____

_____

_____

_____

_____

In the prior section, you thought about how you could blend two of your dharmas/passions together. If they had a baby, what would it be? ☺ For example, two of my passions/purposes are yoga and career coaching. This book and my life purpose coaching philosophy is how I blend them together. How could that look in your own life?

_____

_____

_____

_____

_____

_____

"From every wound there is a scar, and every scar tells a story. A story that says, 'I have survived.'"

—Craig Scott

_____

My top values are (look back to chapter 3 if you need a reminder):

1. _____

2. _____

3. _____

Notice what you are doing here? You're meticulously selecting and assembling the most crucial pieces, creating a clear picture of your calling.

Here's a rather dark but thought-provoking exercise for you: Imagine you've mysteriously vanished from the mortal realm! What would you want to be said in your eulogy? How do you want to be remembered?

_____

_____

_____

_____

_____

_____

_____

_____

BRING IT ALL TOGETHER

Look back at your responses to the reflection prompts above. Reread them and soak it all in. Review your life purpose motto as well.

Now put on your artist hat, pick up your paint brush, and blend them all together. What is all of this leading up to? What do they all have in common?

What is your purpose?

Don't overthink it; just write. From the heart. That is how this process works.

You can't do this wrong.

You got it!

Now, it's time for you to craft your compelling life purpose statement.

MY LIFE PURPOSE IS...

_____

_____

_____

_____

_____

What a masterpiece that is.

Reread it at least a few times. Let it really integrate into the core of your being.

How does that feel, my friend?

I hope you feel a bit clearer now that you have words to put to your purpose.

Take a few deep breaths and feel the connection to yourself. Fully embrace your authentic self.

Repeat these affirmations to yourself:

———————

"I am profoundly in tune with the person I am and the person I'm continually evolving into. I stand prepared to live harmoniously with my genuine life purpose, embracing the fullest potential of my life and career. I greet the future with open arms, welcoming its opportunities. I grant myself the gift of vulnerability and wholeheartedly trust the journey."

———————

Now let's dive a bit deeper.

HOW TO USE YOUR LIFE PURPOSE
MOTTO AND STATEMENT

Now that you have your life purpose motto and statement, these serve as a guiding compass to offer clarity and direction as you entertain various opportunities that come your way. They shine a spotlight on what truly matters and can help you prioritize your path as you navigate through life.

Keep in mind that these statements are not fixed in stone. Like the dynamic individual that you are, ever changing, these life-changing statements will evolve as you do. Leave space for them (and you) to unfold and continue to develop.

BONUS STATEMENTS

"Y'all got any more of that extra credit?"

O VERACHIEVER? HOW DO YOU FEEL about crafting some bonus statements for "extra credit?"

You can apply these statements to other domains in your life. (Remember physical, cognitive, emotional, spiritual?) That could include things like finances, learning, relationships, and spirituality, to name a few.

Let's explore a couple of examples that I wrote myself in my own life, including how I want to show up as a parent and as a partner.

EXAMPLE: MY DHARMA STATEMENT

"I serve as a reminder that we are divine beings capable of manifesting our desires, through skillful intention and concrete action.

I live with strength, grace, integrity, and truth.

I continue to refine my purpose by trusting my intuition, honoring my values, and continuing to exercise my strengths. I support others in the discovery of the integration of mind, body, and spirit and to align with their life purpose."

EXAMPLE: MY PARENTING STATEMENT

"I empower my children to recognize their divine potential, teaching them that they have the ability to manifest their dreams through skillful intention and concrete action.

I guide them with strength, grace, integrity, and truth.

I continue to refine my purpose regarding parenting by trusting my intuition, honoring my values, and continuing to exercise my strengths. I support my children in their discovery of the integration of mind, body, and spirit and to align with their life purpose."

EXAMPLE: MY PARTNER STATEMENT

"My husband and I function as a cohesive unit, bringing our desires into fruition through skillful intention and concrete action.

I honor him with strength, grace, integrity, and truth.

I continually hone my role as a partner by trusting my intuition, honoring my cherished values, and continuing to exercise my strengths. I wholeheartedly assist my husband on his journey towards integrating mind, body, and spirit, and helping him align with his life purpose."

Take a bit of time to digest the exercises you just took part in (and give yourself a pat on the back while you are at it!).

Maybe you want to write some additional statements that may call to you, depending on where you are in life. Here is some space for you to play and imagine:

_____

_____

_____

_____

Melissa M. Carvalho, M.A., RYT

NOW WHAT?

Now you have some words to define your purpose. But living your purpose doesn't just magically unfold. It may require some time for introspection and integration into your daily existence.

You have declared your purpose, but how do you ACTIVATE your purpose? Your purpose ignites when you:

- Embody its intention

- Declare it to others

- Use it as a compass to determine where to direct your energy in life

- Initiate concrete action in alignment with it

Then you can live it.

But this is not easy.

To embody the intention of your purpose, you need to LIVE your purpose's core values. This is where the real work begins.

(And if you're an introvert, don't be too scared.). You don't need to necessarily share it on social or put it in your LinkedIn summary, cover letter, or résumé (but maybe you do!). Hanging it on the wall or telling your best friend or adorable pooch about it works too!

Purpose Forward transcends mere step-by-step guidance; it's a roadmap to transformation. Lists alone can't bring about this level of change. You've chosen this book because you're hungry for transformation and ready to free yourself from the confines that have kept you stuck!

So, it's time to get to work.

Embracing your purpose and translating it into action not only promises fulfillment in your own life and the lives you impact but also plays an integral part in fueling the transformative movement that our world desperately requires at this moment.

Think of it this way: Big accomplishments are made up of many small steps. It starts with your family, the people you work with, and the community you're a part of. Small actions add up to something big. It is how greatness emerges.

Your influence extends, touching others like ripples in a pond, enabling you to connect with a broadening reach.

THIS is the catalyst for instigating positive change and enhancing the world we live in.

It's about declaring and living it, and living it intentionally. It needs to be ALL of our intentions to show up in this way.

You see, we are all part of the same whole. When we normalize talking about our purpose and our personal mission, we normalize a collective awakening, inspiring positive change and connection within our global community, where we all benefit by rising up.

That's precisely why we must take the impact of our purpose-driven lives seriously.

We deserve to thrive in this life; it is our birthright.

Will you rise up to the challenge?

I hope you do.

Because I know you can.

So think about WHY you want to fulfill your purpose and personal mission. The lives it will touch.

Be the change you want to see in the world.

OK, Purpose Seeker, now that you have some super awesome statements to give life to your life story, and to your purpose, let's see about WHAT we do with that to make it activate!

(Are you excited? I know I am!)

MINDFULNESS CORNER
FUTURE SELF MEDITATION

Before you shimmy on over to the next section, where we'll dive into creating an action plan to bring your mission to life, I invite you to take some time for a guided meditation. (This one is a bit longer than the previous ones.) This session will allow you to connect with your future self, and you'll have a little support getting from where you are to where you want to be in the future. It's longer than the rest (over 14 minutes), so I will spare you from reading it all.

Listen here:
https://tinyurl.com/purposeforwardresources

STEP 4

LAUNCHING: WHAT DO I WANT TO DO?

CHAPTER 7

MY NEXT STEPS

"The power of your purpose lies in the concrete actions that support it."

N OW THAT YOU'VE HAD A chance to meet your future self in the prior meditation, let's do the work needed to GET you there!

This chapter is about INTEGRATING your purpose into your daily life through concrete action steps. You've done some great work on getting clear on your life purpose. Now that you have these powerful tools, it's time to own your full potential. It's time to free yourself from any self-imposed limitations of staying small that have kept you from fully thriving. Your roadmap to becoming your fully actualized self is waiting for you!

You may realize that you are ready for your new career, or a new job— but it could be a smaller-scale change that's in your future.

Perhaps realizing your purpose is as simple as adding a little passion project on the side, collaborating with a friend, learning a new skill, or volunteering for a meaningful cause.

It could even mean asking your current supervisor for additional duties that align more with your purpose, or scaling out duties that do not bring you joy.

Again, purpose is not what we do. It's how we show up.

Some ideas of what that could look like:

- If morale needs a boost at work, consider inviting your coworkers to lunch and fostering camaraderie.

- If you value play and creativity, infuse these qualities into your interactions.

- If you wish people would adopt healthier eating habits, offer homemade freeze pops at your next gathering.

Ultimately, it's all about the way you manifest your purpose in your actions.

You may also be inclined to translate your dharma into a professional path, whether it be through a career, a job, or even as a solopreneur or entrepreneur.

I got you!

We are about to investigate the careers, industries, jobs, and organizations that will utilize the skills, passions, and values that you have.

From there, you will come up with a plan to further explore these roles, which will involve connecting with professionals in the field.

In career development, we frequently throw around the stat that 80 percent of job opportunities arise through networking. *Reference: practically every career development office out there!

You will also devise a solid job search strategy that encompasses personal branding and résumé and cover letter enrichments.

But first, you get to step into your "right brain" and have a little creative fun. I'd like you to come up with three **different "vocational plans" for the next five years of your life**.

1. What can I ADD to my current life? This may mean welcoming some tweaks in your current role (or a different role in your current organization) to bring in more purpose, or even adding a new project or volunteer experience on the side.

_____

_____

_____

_____

_____

2. What is my backup plan if I lose my job?

_____

_____

_____

_____

3. This is my dream plan if money were no object:

_____

_____

_____

_____

Take some time to digest these answers. Which of these scenarios above feels the best? I want you to keep these three plans in mind as we move into the next section. You don't necessarily need to pick one now. But the answer may slowly become clearer as you explore potential options.

REFLECTION

Go back and revisit your life purpose statement. Notice how it resonates with you.

Is it genuine and realistic? It's crucial to honestly evaluate if anything might be holding you back from realizing it—whether that's resistance, limiting beliefs, or fear. These obstacles can manifest in various aspects of your life, including attitudes, belief systems, behavior patterns, routines, negative influences, career, health, and spirituality.

It might be worth revisiting the sections on conditioning, self-esteem, and self-care. Is there additional work needed in these areas before you're fully prepared to embrace your purpose? Recognizing and addressing these aspects is a potent tool on your journey toward becoming the dharma-activated human I know you are!

Does anything come up for you here?

_____

_____

_____

_____

_____

_____

MANIFEST YOUR INTENTION LIKE A PRO

Before you bop over to the next section, close your eyes, put your hand on your heart, and feel your self-worth. Take three deep cleansing breaths, breathing in for 4, pausing for 4, and exhaling for 6. Feel your sense of purpose and the heartfelt intention that drives it. Take a few moments to reflect on WHY you want to fulfill your purpose. How will it affect your family, your community, or the world at large?

_____

_____

_____

_____

_____

_____

Now that you have your purposeful intention, what *high-vibration attitude* (uplifting mindset and energy) can you connect with that intention to enhance it? (Think gratitude, joy, love, creativity, abundance, peace, compassion, hope, community, etc.) When you tune into the energy the future holds for you, you draw it closer with greater intensity. Identify four high-vibration attitudes to infuse into your intention to manifest your purpose-driven life.

1. _____

2. _____

3. _____

4. _____

There. Now let's explore some concrete vocational options that could be viable choices for you.

VOCATIONAL
EXPLORATION

"Ask what makes you come alive, and go do it. Because what the world needs is people who have come alive."

—Howard Thurman

M Y HOPE IS THAT YOU may be feeling a tad bit clearer about what your purpose IS, and maybe you're even getting some ideas of how you can seamlessly align your purpose with a career path or passion project. Remember, it doesn't need to necessarily manifest in the form of a full-time job (at least not right away, or perhaps not at all). It could look like volunteering for the local animal shelter, posting on social about creative ways to educate others, writing a book on gardening, enrolling in a new class, or even pursuing a side hustle like baking.

Note: For ease of communicating, I will frequently use the words "vocation" or "career," but know that this word can easily be replaced with "volunteer role," "part-time job," "gig," "project," "passion," etc. You choose your word! ☺

VOCATIONAL INVESTIGATION MAP

Let's look at a diagram I created to help you zero in on some important factors to keep in mind when considering vocational options. Think back to your strengths and passions. In what ways can you artfully blend them together to find some options that utilize them both? Options that people will pay a decent amount for (I am guessing in a perfect world, you may want to make a little cheddar, right?!). That's the trick!

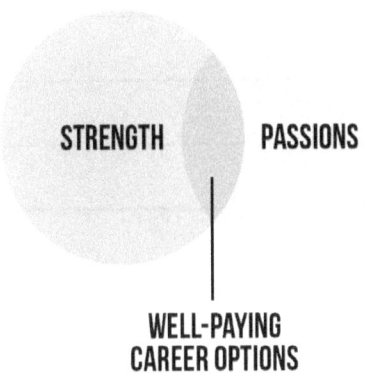

STRENGTH   **PASSIONS**

WELL-PAYING CAREER OPTIONS

Here is an exercise to assist in that goal:

My Top Strengths/Skills	My Top Passions

Now find the common ground. What connections exist between the columns? What types of roles could be born out of these parts of yourself (that can also potentially pay decently, if that is important to you—and usually it is!)?

1. _____

2. _____

3. _____

4. _____

5. _____

You may very well already have some of the concrete options above. (If you do, that's friggen' awesome, and I am so genuinely excited for you!) If you still need more, no worries; I have plenty more to offer to help get you there.

We will now explore "career clusters," which group occupations together that share common skills. This will help to not only reveal professions with similar skillsets but also help in gaining insight into potential *industries* you might enjoy as well. Following this, we will take a look at individual job roles and even pinpoint specific organizations to target.

SAMPLE CAREER CLUSTERS
(CAREERS THAT SHARE COMMON SKILLS)
PULLED FROM ONET ONLINE

Highlight or circle the ones above that most resonate with you (perhaps 2–3).

Agriculture, Food, and Natural Resources
Architecture and Construction
Arts, Audio/Visual Technology, and Communications

Business, Management, and Administration
Education and Training
Finance
Government and Public Administration
Health Science
Hospitality and Tourism
Human Services
Information Technology
Law, Public Safety, Corrections, and Security
Manufacturing
Marketing
Science, Technology, Engineering, and Mathematics (STEM)
Transportation, Distribution, and Logistics
Other (write it here): _____
Other (write it here): _____

How did that feel?

Now that you have a few career clusters to investigate, look up the various types of careers associated with them here on the ONET: https://tinyurl.com/purposeforwardresources

This is a pretty cool site that will connect you to a list of careers that you can research in depth, including the tasks that the role includes, projected growth in the next year, skills and training needed, average pay, and related occupations. Spend some time investigating here.

Notice what occupations catch your eye. You may even want to revisit some of the careers that are connected to your MBTI type that looked interesting to you—refer to chapter 2 and investigate these as well.

Be sure to pay special attention to the related occupations. Keep note of the job titles, projected growth rates, median wages, skills you already have, and any education/skills you may need to acquire. Grab the Target Role Worksheet here: https://tinyurl.com/purposeforwardresources

Target role notes:

_____

_____

_____

_____

_____

_____

Now that you have some specific roles to target, it's time to research some real-life job postings! You will be amazed at how much clarity comes from reading real-life postings. Go to your favorite job search website (Indeed, Glassdoor, ZipRecruiter, LinkedIn, etc.) and look up some roles that interest you. Notice the types of job titles they are using and the industries they are tied to, as well as the job duties and requirements.

Another thing to take note of is the keywords that the posting uses. These are the specific terms and phrases that employers use to identify the essential skills, qualifications, and experiences they're seeking in a strong candidate.

Some examples may be programming languages, data analysis, project management, graphic design, web development, mechanical engineering, foreign languages, and more.

The keywords will come in handy later, when it's time to write your résumé and cover letter.

While you do this research, note the following:

- The most eye-catching roles

- The job duties and keywords that are mentioned

- The education/training and experience required

- The ideal type of organization you are drawn to—public, private, nonprofit, government, startup, etc.

- The industry it is in (i.e., technology, healthcare, renewable energy, etc.)

- The culture of the organization (i.e., diversity-focused, fast-paced, very corporate, etc.)

- Your favorite employers

Feel free to grab my Job Log Sheet here: https://tinyurl.com/purposeforwardresources to document the organizations, roles, skills, and keywords they require.

Job posting research notes:

_____

_____

_____

_____

_____

Take a moment to notice if there are any gaps between the types of roles that interest you and the education/skills/experience they require. It's possible that you'll need to explore avenues for gaining some more related experience through volunteering, taking on a side project, enrolling in a course, or developing new skills.

In fact, you may even consider investing in your personal and professional growth by engaging the services of a seasoned career coach. They can offer invaluable assistance in crafting a personalized, robust action plan, holding you accountable, and giving you the support you need! ☺

Great job! I know you're starting to get excited to explore these options a bit more, and maybe you're even beginning to visualize yourself in some of these roles. Now, let's delve into the art of building connections to gather valuable insights. This involves engaging in conversations with industry peers and mentors and, if possible, shadowing their work experiences. Let's explore.

CONNECTING AND JOB SEARCH STRATEGY

The trick to good networking is to forget there is any-thing you are looking to get. Just give instead.

NOW THAT YOU HAVE A list of some potential career options, the next step is to reach out to people who do similar work to find out more about it and see if it may be a good fit for you. We will discuss what those conversations will look like.

So, who do you reach out to? Think in terms of the "first-degree" connections you have—family, friends, neighbors, contacts from organizations, or various places you have worked. Those first-degree connections can also introduce you to connections they have in the field as well.

In addition to starting with your current connections, we can also explore how you can leverage LinkedIn to reach out to people you DON'T yet know, but who can help you on your journey.

Yes, it's about to get REAL now! We are not just writing our hopes and dreams down on paper. It's time to DO something with them.

Does that scare you?

If it does, you are normal.

Just remember that getting out of your comfort zone is how transformation happens. ☺

By connecting with others in your potential field, you can find out more and determine if these are areas (and potential organizations) you'd like to explore further.

This section could easily be called "networking," but I have discovered that this word often carries negative associations— intimidating, scary, and just too much pressure. In reality, it's about connecting with people, getting to know them better, sharing your interests and aspirations, and finding ways to help each other. It can be as simple as connecting someone's daughter with the perfect gymnastics studio, recommending a great book, or introducing them to someone who can help them move closer to their goals.

And yes—it can lead to an interview and, ultimately, a job offer!

So where exactly do you go to connect with these people?

It's all about discovering your community and finding your tribe. Here's a list of potential places to explore:

- Use LinkedIn (professional social networking platform) to connect with individuals in specific roles or fields and consider joining relevant groups.

- Explore podcasts where professionals share their experiences and expertise.

- Engage with Facebook groups that focus on your areas of interest.

- Join professional networking groups designed for career growth.

- Check out events on platforms like Eventbrite.

- Get involved with your local chamber of commerce for business- and career-related opportunities.

- Utilize Google to search for relevant communities and events.

- Reconnect with your alma mater, both your high school and college, for alumni networks and events.

- Attend job fairs where you can meet potential employers and peers.

- Attend Meetup groups.

- Look for targeted networking events that align with your career aspirations.

SAMPLE LINKEDIN MESSAGE TO THOSE YOU WOULD LIKE TO CONNECT WITH

Send a "request" with this message:

"Hi ___! I love the (role) work you are doing at (company) and would enjoy being a part of your network."

Once they add you, here's how to respond:

"Thanks so much for the add! I'm exploring a new career path for myself in (industry) and feel like you would have a lot of insight to offer. (Ask a question or two about the industry). Would you be willing to hop on a call with me at some point for 15–20 minutes so I can pick your brain?"

SAMPLE LINKEDIN MESSAGE TO FOLLOW UP AFTER YOU HAVE APPLIED FOR A JOB

Look to see if the hiring manager or recruiter is listed on the posting. (If this is not the case, find a recruiter within the company.)

Send a "request" with this message:

"Hi ___! I love the (role) work you are doing at (company) and would enjoy being a part of your network."

Once they add you, here's how to respond:

"Thanks so much for the add! I just applied for the (role) position at (company). I have a lot to offer in this role with my (list some of your experience and strengths). Please keep a lookout for my application. I would welcome an opportunity to connect regarding this role and see how I can contribute to your organization."

These are just a few options, and there are many more places where you can connect with people who share your passions and ambitions.

Take a few moments to brainstorm and research some places where your "tribe" may be hanging out. (Go ahead, I'll wait! ☺)

1. _____

2. _____

3. _____

4. _____

5. _____

After you've had the opportunity to dive into these groups, give yourself the freedom to actively participate in these experiences. Embrace your curiosity about the shared traits and the unique culture within these communities. When individuals with common interests and groups come together, they generate a specific and unique energy, and you hold the potential to co-create together.

Allow yourself to pursue connections and continue to nurture them so they continue to evolve. I created a Connections Log sheet to help keep track of your conversations. Access it here: https://tinyurl.com/purposeforwardresources

(If you are anything like me, after a while, it can get hard to remember what conversation you had with who!)

While you connect, be open to the following types of experiences:

METHODS TO EXPLORE CAREER PATHWAYS: CONNECTING, LEARNING, AND GROWING

Mentorship—Connecting with someone more seasoned in the field who can support you in your personal and professional development, helping you to learn and grow. This is especially helpful early on in your career, but useful all throughout!

Peer Support—Engaging with others who have similar career experiences and interests, to learn and grow with each other.

Informational Interviews—A conversation with a professional who works in your career of interest. The goal is to gather information, insights, and advice about that career path, to ultimately help you make informed decisions!

Here are some sample informational interview questions:

- What has your own career journey been like, and what aspects of your education or training have been most instrumental in your current success?

- Can you describe what a recent day at work was like for you?

- What do you like about your job? What do you dislike?

- How is this job and field continuing to evolve?

- What factors turned out to be crucial to success that you weren't expecting?

- Do you have any advice for someone starting in this field or recommendations for further resources or people to connect with?

Job shadowing—This is when you spend time observing a professional in their workplace. The purpose is to understand the daily tasks and get a feel for the work environment, to see if it is something you would enjoy. It can also provide valuable exposure and networking opportunities.

As you connect with professionals and explore various career pathways through these avenues, it's helpful to gather additional valuable information that will guide your job search strategy. Let's chat about the insights you will need that will serve as the foundation for aligning your career goals with the right opportunities for you.

JOB SEARCH STRATEGY

As you engage in connections through the various methods above, here is some essential information to gather, regarding your non-negotiables and preferences that lead the way for your job search strategy:

"Must-Haves" and "Would Like to Haves"

- The values that the field/organization prioritizes

- Preferred location, whether it's a particular a city/town, or whether the work is in person, remote, or hybrid

- Determining the type of organization- public, private, nonprofit, government, etc.

- Size of organization

- Targeted salary range

- Future growth opportunities

These factors will help you align your career goals with the right opportunities for you!

After you have a chance to connect with some of these individuals be sure to log your own personal "Must-Haves" and "Would Like to Haves."

Must-Haves:

_____

_____

_____

_____

_____

Would Like to Haves:

_____

_____

_____

_____

_____

Now that you are clear on what your ideal role would look like, it's time to job search!

Remember that handy job log sheet you created? It may be a nice time to revisit it and possibly even begin to apply to some of the roles! Just go ahead and add the "date applied" to the notes section.

Besides your "must-haves" and "would like to haves," here are some other factors you will want to think about:

What target job search sites do you want to frequent?

_____

_____

_____

What target job titles are you after?

_____

_____

_____

_____

_____

GOAL/INTENTION SETTING

You will also want to think about what your goals are. Are there a certain number of jobs you would like to apply to each week or each month? A certain number of networking connections you would like to make?

Also, be sure to harness your networking powers AFTER you apply for a job as well. Consider reaching out to the hiring manager via LinkedIn or engaging with other professionals in the HR department. If the job is posted on LinkedIn, often it is connected right to the hiring manager's profile. You can also do a search for employees at a certain organization and reach out to them by messaging them and engaging them in conversation about the organization/role/culture and show how your skills connect to it. Your post-application networking can be just as vital as the initial steps in your job search.

Remember how I mentioned earlier that 80 percent of job opportunities come through networking?! This statistic holds true. Your chances of securing a job are significantly higher when it's a result of a personal connection you've nurtured, rather than just submitting applications blindly. Give it a try and witness the results for yourself!

Now that you have gained clarity on some potential career options, go ahead and STATE exactly what your ideal career is. The answer may organically come to you; if you need more inspiration, no worries—the next section will assist you in creating your very own personal mission statement.

Take a moment here to get clear on your intention. When we put words to our intention, it gets clearer. (Bonus points if you tell someone about it!)

My career intention is:

_____

_____

_____

_____

_____

_____

_____

_____

_____

_____

_____

_____

Nice job on stating what you plan to bring to fruition! It's personal branding time.

CHAPTER 8

MY PERSONAL BRAND

*"Do not wish to be anything but what you
are, and try to be that perfectly."*

—Saint Francis de Sales

H ERE WE ARE GOING TO get into personal branding,
which is the art of presenting yourself to the world
to attract the kind of opportunities you desire.
Personal branding reflects your unique identity and empowers
you to tell your personal story.

Your brand image begins with crafting a mission statement.
We will eventually determine how your brand translates to
a résumé, cover letter, your LinkedIn profile, and even your
interviewing skills! (Did I mention when you finish this book,
it comes with a degree in marketing?!) ☺

MY PERSONAL MISSION
STATEMENT

"How do you know if your mission in life is finished? If you're still alive, it isn't."

—Richard Bach

Y OUR PERSONAL MISSION STATEMENT SERVES as the driving force behind your life purpose. It gets into the specifics of how you will "deliver" your life purpose. This statement is especially important if you are interested in entrepreneurship/solopreneurship, but it is equally relevant if you are pursuing a more conventional career path working for someone else.

Alright, take a peek back at your purpose motto from chapter 6—we are going to elevate it into your personal mission statement. (Yes, I am really asking you to write another statement. Can you believe the nerve?!)

This is where you get to declare in greater detail what your purpose entails, who it's for, how exactly you will deliver it, and the impact you hope it will have. It is the more direct and action-oriented manifestation of your life purpose. So essentially, you are taking your life purpose statement and making it more specific so you can impact change. ☺

It infuses it with the HOW, instead of just the WHAT.

Here is the magic formula. Ready?!

I (life purpose motto <action verb/value>) for (audience) by (skills). I provide (service) to (desired impact)

Here is an example:

"I activate purpose *(life purpose motto <action verb/value>)* for career starters *(audience)* by using my intuition and action mindset *(skills)*. I provide life purpose and career coaching *(service)* to confidently launch them into aligning with their fullest life and career potential *(desired impact)*."

Here are some more examples to get you inspired to create your own:

PERSONAL MISSION STATEMENT EXAMPLES

"I facilitate deep personal growth for individuals navigating life transitions by applying my expertise in psychology and active listening skills. I do this by providing compassionate counseling services that empower them to overcome challenges and achieve emotional well-being and personal growth."

—Melissa

"I champion mental health awareness for teenagers by leveraging my storytelling and public speaking skills. I provide engaging talks and open discussions to promote understanding and emotional well-being among adolescents."

—Bridget

"I transform wellness for busy professionals by combining my knowledge of exercise physiology and motivational techniques. I provide personalized fitness guidance to help them achieve their health goals and cultivate a sustainable, active lifestyle."

—Chuck

"I uplift the spirits of hospitalized children by entertaining them with my magical performances. I provide interactive magic shows to bring joy and laughter into their challenging circumstances."

—Alisha

Now it's your turn. Use your own words. Make sure it really sounds like you!

MY PERSONAL MISSION STATEMENT IS:

_____

_____

_____

_____

_____

_____

Good effort! What you've created is pretty rad, and it's bound to leave a profound impact on the lives that you touch.

Now let's see how this can plug into the "toolkit" we will use to get who we are out into the world.

PERSONAL BRANDING

"Whatever you are, be a good one!"

—William Makepeace Thackeray

B Y NOW, YOU HOPEFULLY HAVE a clearer sense of who you are, what you want, and how you are going to get there. This is the part where you get to take all of that and showcase your authentic self and all that you have to offer an employer.

Now you are ready to assemble your personalized "job acquisition toolkit," and it's far from solely the mundane résumés and cover letters that everyone else submits as "good enough." No, dear purpose-driven seeker, this is your chance to serve your truest and most exceptional self on a silver platter to the world—a self that embodies your life purpose.

And you, my fellow purpose-seeker, won't accept anything less!

Staying in alignment with my own life purpose and the core mission of this book, the emphasis here is on the journey of uncovering and wholeheartedly embracing your life purpose rather than focusing on résumé writing. I need to acknowledge that this section is an especially challenging one for me to write, because this section alone could easily be an entire book or two.

But I came up with a solution that I believe will bring satisfaction to us all. I have put together a treasure trove of valuable resources to support you. It will highlight a collection of my personally endorsed books and resources, each directly relevant to the topics we cover here. So, if you want more, knock yourself out! You can find it here (as well as at the end of the book): https://www.melissamcarvalho. com/purposeforwardresources

You've already come up with your mission statement, which is the foundational element of your personal brand. Now let's explore how we can seamlessly integrate this core message into your résumé, LinkedIn profile, cover letter, and interviewing strategy.

Let's begin.

MY RÉSUMÉ

Your résumé should represent your purpose, highlighting the elements that mean the most to you.

- **Define your purpose.** Your résumé should not just list your past positions but illustrate the impact you've had and how it resonates with your purpose. This can be done in a profile or summary section at the top of the résumé that conveys your passion and the impact you want to make in your field.

- **Show off your achievements.** Don't just list job responsibilities. Highlight the specific achievements you've made. Have them show how your work has contributed to your own personal growth and fulfillment. You may even want to have an "accomplishments" or "strengths" section before your work experience to highlight your achievements.

- **Tailor your résumé to each role you apply for.** Align your skills and experience with the specific requirements for each role you are applying for. Yes, this means you will have lots and lots of résumé versions on your laptop! Your résumé is also not a list of everything you have ever done. Just those things that are most recent (within the past 10 years) and relevant.

Notes:

_____

_____

_____

_____

_____

_____

MY LINKEDIN PROFILE

LinkedIn is your digital professional identity, and it's a powerful tool for connecting your personal brand to your life purpose and career aspirations. You want to create a LinkedIn profile that effectively represents your personal brand and ties it into your life purpose and career goals.

- **Professional profile picture:** People want to know that they are talking to a real, live, awesome person—you! Post a high-quality, professional photo as your profile pic. You want to make a strong first impression.

- **Personalized headline and summary:** Make sure these sections on your profile say more than just a job title. Have them convey expertise and passion. Show your personality. Add your compelling narrative to your summary section so that it tells the story of your career journey and how it connects to your broader mission. Let your personality shine through. Connect it all to your mission.

- **Keyword optimization:** It is so very important to use the relevant keywords throughout your profile, especially in the summary and experience sections. This will make it easier for your future employers to find you! (Need a refresher on what keywords are? Look back to the "Vocational Exploration" section.)

Notes:

_____

_____

_____

_____

_____

_____

MY COVER LETTER

This is your chance to let some of your authenticity and passion come through, emphasizing the alignment between your mission and the organization's mission.

- **Have a strong first paragraph.** Begin with an enticing opening that clearly demonstrates your passion and purpose. Share a brief personal story or experience that connects your personal mission to the role you are applying to. This can immediately engage your future boss and put you at the top of the pile (and there will be competition!).

- **Show how you align with the company's mission.** Research the company's mission, vision, values, and culture. Highlight how your own mission and values align with those of the company. Emphasize the impact you hope to make within the organization and how it resonates with your life purpose.

- **Draw attention to your impact and results.** In the body of the cover letter, highlight specific examples from your past experiences that demonstrate how you've worked towards your goals and achieved results. Use concrete, quantifiable achievements to illustrate your impact.

Notes:

_____

_____

_____

_____

_____

_____

_____

MY INTERVIEW STRATEGY

Interviews can be anxiety-provoking, but remember, practice makes perfect. As you step into interviews, authenticity is key. Show how your values and goals align with the role and the organization's mission.

- **Self-reflection.** Spend significant time researching the organization and the role before the interview. Explore how the role aligns with your own passions, values, skills, and ultimately, your life purpose. This self-awareness will help you to speak authentically during the interview. And authenticity is vital!

- **Frame your experiences as stories.** Don't just respond with one-sentence answers. Respond to questions as a narrative that reflects your purpose and mission. Share how you've grown, what you've learned, and how this job opportunity fits into your overall life journey.

- **Ask Purposeful Questions.** This is a big one. It demonstrates your genuine interest, curiosity, and strategic thinking. You will also gather valuable insights about the company and role, helping to ensure a strong fit and alignment of your values and goals with the organization's.

Notes:

_____

_____

_____

_____

_____

_____

_____

Whew! From self-exploration to career exploration to career liftoff, we have been through a lot together, haven't we?!

It doesn't seem like it was too long ago that you cracked open this book, unsure that any answers about your future would become clear.

I am sincerely grateful that you stuck with it.

Now that you have a shiny new personal brand ready to show off, let's give you the last dose of purpose medicine. The last bit of inspiration to take your purpose-driven life across the finish line, where you'll authentically "Purpose Forward."

STEP 5

LIVING (AND DECLARING) MY PURPOSE!

CHAPTER 9

PURPOSE FORWARD

Discovering and embracing your purpose is not just a transformative journey for yourself; it ripples through time, leaving an imprint on the generations that follow.

Y OU'VE BEEN ON QUITE A journey, Purpose Seeker! You came into this unclear about what your future aspirations were and how you were going to get there.

You have taken the time for self-reflection by gathering the tools you need to venture out and live your dharma, including a deeper understanding of your personality, roles, archetypes, limiting beliefs, and childhood conditioning.

- You've found clarity on your passions, values, and strengths.

- You have taken various assessments to give you insight on who you are, including the MBTI, Holland Code, and StrengthsFinder.

- You have learned to value self-care and the importance it has in setting the foundation for living a life of purpose. You have taken part in reflection and guided meditations regarding the physical, cognitive, emotional, and spiritual domains and how they connect to the eight life areas, including your relationships, health, career, finances, spirituality, recreation, community, and self-development.

- You have put powerful words together to form a life purpose statement, a personal mission statement, and more.

- You have explored various career paths, learned how to connect with others who do the work you want to do, and maybe even took part in an experiential experience such as a job shadow.

- You created a personal brand to distinguish your unique qualities that plugs into your resume, cover letter, and LinkedIn profile.

- You have come out the other side with clear intentions, goals, and a positive mindset.

What you've taken the time to do will prove to be a transformative life experience that I hope will bring you tremendous pride and fulfillment.

So take a moment to put your hand on your heart and give gratitude to yourself.

You deserve to celebrate this moment. (Know that I am celebrating you too!)

All that's left to do is go out and do it—LIVE your purpose. And that's what it's all about.

I leave you with these last few points:

Purpose is not what you do. It's how you show up. It may not manifest as a career. It may very well be pursuing a passion or side project, or caring for someone who needs it.

The goal is to log those purpose hours.

Whatever that may look like.

Even if it is just a few hours a week. Find what you are passionate about; read about it, speak about it, volunteer for it. Just being in the same space as others who can benefit from your passions is living your purpose. Those few hours a week will really add up over the course of a month, year, or lifetime.

So, I ask you, what might that look like in your life? What can you commit to doing, even if it's just three hours a week?

_____

_____

_____

_____

Find the passions that exist inside you that light you up—and go do it! Show up in that way every single day. By doing this, you are ensuring that you are unequivocally embracing and embodying your authentic purpose.

PURPOSING FORWARD

Finding and embracing your life purpose isn't just about changing your own life; it also leaves a mark on the generations to come. When you discover your purpose, you're like a trailblazer, showing the way to those who'll follow. Parents who live a life of prioritizing their purpose serve as an inspirational model to their children for how to do the same. Embracing your purpose makes you a force for empowerment that will continue to uplift fellow humans for years (and maybe even generations) to come.

The power lies within you.

Now it's time to step forward boldly and magnify your dedication to living and vocalizing your purpose. It is a covenant with your community and a promise to yourself, affirming that you will allow your purpose to occupy the space in your life that it rightfully deserves.

Say the following out loud or to yourself (or even write your own!):

THE "PURPOSE FORWARD" PROMISE

I live a life
Of intentional purpose.
It is my sacred responsibility
To show up
As my authentic, purpose-driven self.
What that looks like can shift from day to day.
I accept all of this.
I will give what I have to give.
And I will take care of myself holistically
Every step of the way.

I will stumble and I will fall.
Adversity will test me.
But I will rise
And I will go on.

I choose to nurture my calling now
Because the "now" is all that truly exists.

I am grateful for the Energy of Purpose
And my connection to it.
I release any negative thoughts
That keep me from

Manifesting my dharma.

I will allow my purpose to evolve as I evolve.
Following the path
That continuously returns me
To who I truly am.

My purpose integrates with the world's purpose.
It is my duty to do my part.

I will surround myself with others
who are living lives of purpose
and reassure them along their way.
I will seek to inspire others
who need the "purpose spark" ignited within them.

I humbly resolve
To actively choose
To give my best every day
And to live my purpose.

MY WISH FOR YOU:

May you be blessed with the wisdom

To know who you are

To spread your light

And manifest your desires.

May you live from a place of creativity and curiosity

And dive deeper to understand

The essence of who you truly are

Where you have been

And where you are led.

Namaste.

I have just one last question for you:

Will you resolve to live your purpose?

LET'S KEEP THIS GOING!

I AM HONORED THAT YOU HAVE chosen to take this journey with me.

INVEST IN YOURSELF AND YOUR PURPOSE!

I offer individual coaching sessions (a discovery call is free!), group coaching sessions, and Transformational Purpose Retreats. Email me at melissa@melissamcarvalho.com to find out more.

I INVITE YOU TO STAY CONNECTED:

Website:
https://www.melissamcarvalho.com/

LinkedIn:
https://www.linkedin.com/in/melissamarycarvalho/

Facebook:
https://www.facebook.com/MelissaCarvalhoPurpose/

Email:
melissa@melissamcarvalho.com

JOIN THE PURPOSE FORWARD MOVEMENT!

Get access to all the Purpose Forward resources, including assessments, meditations, links, and real-life people's dharma statements, here: https://www.melissamcarvalho. com/purposeforwardresources.

You can even upload your very own life purpose statement (and picture, if you wish). You may even be chosen to be highlighted on social media!

TAKE YOGA WITH ME!

Offering yoga in the park, virtual yoga, and retreats!

https://www.melissamcarvalho.com/ melissacarvalhoyoga

SHARE THE LOVE!

Could your team, organization, book club, or group benefit from Purpose work? I have a limited number of speaking engagements, retreats, and workshops/seminars available. Exclusive bulk discounts on the book are also available. Reach out to melissa@melissamcarvalho.com for more!

Know someone else who can benefit from Purpose work? Please recommend this book to them and help us get more Purpose Seekers in our tribe!

I'd be incredibly grateful if you could take a moment to share your thoughts and leave a review for my book.

Melissa M. Carvalho, M.A., RYT

RECOMMENDED READING & RESOURCES

Get more readings and resources on these topics:

✓ Career exploration

✓ Resume preparation

✓ Interviewing

✓ Career meditations

✓ Self-care

And more!

https://www.melissamcarvalho.com/purposeforwardresources

ACKNOWLEDGMENTS

T O THE MIGHTY TRIBE OF individuals who helped bring this book to fruition: It truly would not exist without you.

To the intuitive healer who gave me energy work at Kripalu Center for Yoga in March of 2023 and announced to me upon arrival with complete confidence, sentiment, and curiosity that I have "a baby in me"—you were right... I did. I knew exactly what you meant. I had this book in me, just waiting to be born. ♥

Thank you for delivering that significant message to me and being the catalyst to give me the assurance to acknowledge that, put action to it, and ultimately birth it. This book would not exist without you.

To my husband, my Johnny—my rock, and my love. To my first-round editor, who meticulously went through every word on several occasions, pushing me to produce the best possible version—I owe so much to you. Including teaching me to love in a way I never knew was possible. For being my life partner, a constant support, and the bridge to making all my dreams come true. I love co-creating life with you. Endless gratitude to all you give to me, and your family, every day.

I would again like to express endless gratitude to my mother, Mary Jaroma Misiaszek, for living a life of wild devotion to her passions. It is because of you that I learned what life purpose truly is. And to the maternal line of strong women who preceded us both—women who boldly pursued their career purpose and education when it was rare for our gender to do so, as midwives and math professors, among other noble professions—I am deeply humbled by the immense privilege I have been given, and it is my life's work to pay forward your legacy. I know that it is *your* DNA that empowers me to fearlessly birth what I carry within—purpose.

To my father, Gary John Misiaszek: Through osmosis, you have taught me the strong values of discipline, hard work, and commitment to all endeavors and relationships in life. It was at the times I wanted to give up that I straightened my crown, remembered where I came from, and got back to it. I learned that from you. ☺

Endless gratitude to Coral Brown, my therapist and coach, who introduced me to the concept of a dharma statement. It is because of you and that simple exercise that I opened my mind up to a world of intentional purpose. This book would never exist without you, and there is not a day that goes by that I am not grateful for you sharing this empowering and life-changing practice with me.

Demetria Moran, I will always cherish the immense quality of career development inspiration I acquired under your leadership. Thank you for choosing me and taking a chance on me. Thank you for being the best mentor a girl could ever ask for. You will always hold a very special place in my heart.

I wouldn't have gotten this far without the expertise and encouragement from my book coach and editor, Dan Tortora. Thank you for talking me through each step of the process, teaching me to write like a pro, and keeping me calm as a cucumber throughout. You have gone above and beyond, and I have endless gratitude for the gifts you share.

To my grandmother, Dolly Ducharme Misiaszek, who I have the privilege of having a beautiful relationship with, being just 47 years apart. Your unconditional love, support, and holding the space for me to process the journey that is life has helped to shape me into the woman I am today. I am grateful for your unwavering presence and love. I am forever appreciative of our time together and the ways you continue to shape me.

And finally, to my cherished daughters Samantha and Abigail, your zest for life has challenged me to dig even deeper for purpose. You are a constant reminder that each one of us is worthy of a joyful existence. I love you beyond measure and am deeply grateful that you have chosen me to be your mother. I hope I make you proud. My deepest wish for you is that you remember that you are worthy to unapologetically chase and acquire your deepest desires.

Heartfelt gratitude to everyone who has contributed to bringing this book to life and has shown unwavering support. An extra special thanks to my clients and yoga students, whose daily inspiration is truly an honor. Serving you is a privilege, and I am grateful for each and every one of you.

Purpose Forward.

ABOUT THE AUTHOR

 Melissa Carvalho, M.A., RYT is a holistic life purpose & career coach, Fortune 300 recruiter, and a yoga teacher. She is a talent development expert with over 15 years of experience, as well as an adjunct professor at Rhode Island College.

She created the *Purpose Forward Program* in 2020 and has been meticulously refining it ever since!

She lives in Rhode Island with her husband, two energetic daughters, and adventurous cat Cindy Lou (who once went missing but was reunited with her family with the help of a pet detective!)

Visit www.melissamcarvalho.com to learn more about Melissa's work—and why she believes you deserve to live a life of purpose.